Victims of Crime and Community Justice

Victims of Crime and Community Justice

Brian Williams

Jessica Kingsley Publishers
London and Philadelphia

First published in 2005
by Jessica Kingsley Publishers
116 Pentonville Road
London N1 9JB, UK
and
400 Market Street, Suite 400
Philadelphia, PA 19106, USA

www.jkp.com

Library of Congress Cataloging in Publication Data

Williams, Brian, 1953-
    Victims of crime and community justice / Brian Williams.-- 1st American paperback ed.
        p. cm.
    Includes bibliographical references and index.
    ISBN-13: 978-1-84310-195-6 (pbk.)
    ISBN-10: 1-84310-195-5 (pbk.)
    1. Victims of crimes--Government policy--Great Britain. 2. Restorative justice--Great Britain. 3. Criminal justice, Administration of--Great Britain. I. Title.
    HV6250.3.G7W55 2005
    362.88'0941--dc22
                            2005001702

British Library Cataloguing in Publication Data
A CIP catalogue record for this book is available from the British Library

ISBN-13: 978 1 84310 195 6
ISBN-10: 1 84310 195 5

Printed and bound in Great Britain by
Athenaeum Press, Gateshead, Tyne and Wear

Contents

Acknowledgements

First of all, I would like to thank the library staff at the Kimberlin Library at De Montfort University for their tireless and enthusiastic help: in particular Sue Beardsmore, Sally Luxton and the inter-library loan staff have been of great assistance.

Help with particular issues and sources of material was received from a range of people, and in particular I owe gratitude to Denis Bracken, Carole Clark, Krystyna Findley, Hannah Goodman, Elliot Juby, Jan Kilgallon, Gill Mackenzie, Mike Nellis, Kieran O'Dwyer, Bas van Stokkom, Sandra Walklate, Elisabeth Wynhoff and Joe Yates.

Students on my MA module on 'Working with Victims of Crime' provided stimulus and raised (and often answered) questions which assisted with the development of my ideas in the course of preparing the book, and I am grateful to them.

I am extremely fortunate in working with a supportive and committed group of colleagues in the Community and Criminal Justice Research Centre at De Montfort University, and I would like to record my thanks to all of them for their understanding, advice and collegial support.

The first part of Chapter Two expands upon an article first published as an editorial in the *British Journal of Community Justice* in 2002. I have been influenced and assisted by the responses that article in particular and the journal in general have received in the period since then.

Some of the case studies in Chapter Four are expanded versions of material from my chapter in Hale *et al.* (Williams forthcoming). The case study of Alenka in Chapter Six is an expanded and updated version of case material used in my inaugural professorial lecture at De Montfort University on 27 March 2003, which in turn drew upon important journalistic research by Vulliamy (2004) and Gibb (2003).

Suzanne Williams has been a constant source of encouragement and support throughout the preparation of the book. Adam has no idea why I disappear to work in the attic for days on end, but he has been very good about it. Siân's arrival disrupted and delayed things a little, but she deserves thanks for ensuring that the book is topical and up-to-date.

Brian Williams

Chapter One

Introduction

Outline of the book

Victims of crime were of little concern to legislators and policymakers world-wide as recently as the 1960s, but in many jurisdictions their interests are now seen as crucial. This book aims to describe and explain the processes which have been involved in creating this change, and to raise some questions about the genuineness of the current apparent policy interest in victim issues. Organisations claiming to represent victims have become increasingly vocal and influential over this period and in the process the issues involved have inevitably been politicised: some of the advantages and drawbacks of this development are discussed in this chapter, along with a brief and selective history of victim policy internationally, which aims to show how certain common themes have dominated the development of this area of policy.

Chapter Two considers community justice, its meanings and its implications for victims, drawing upon examples from a number of countries. Like so many developments in criminal justice, the movement towards community justice has at times failed to consider victims' needs sufficiently, despite its ostensible aim of encouraging the return of the 'ownership' of criminal justice to those most affected by its decisions.

In Chapter Three, the rise of restorative justice is considered. Different models of restorative justice have evolved in various countries, and this has implications for victims of crime whose involvement and responses are likely to vary according to the approaches taken. Here again, the need to balance the interests of the various parties appropriately is a major concern. In a number of countries, restorative justice has been introduced in an attempt to deal with growing public disquiet about the operation of conventional criminal justice. In many cases, reform has been *offender-led*, in the sense that it has arisen from concern about how to rehabilitate offenders more successfully rather than from a desire to deal more appropriately and compassionately with victims. As a result, the system tends to concentrate on punishing, changing and rehabilitating offenders; victims are sometimes called upon to assist with these aims rather than receiving recognition of their potentially central role in the criminal justice process. This has led to considerable reluctance by victims to become involved in some initiatives, although participation rates have been relatively high elsewhere. Despite the problems encountered in a number of jurisdictions, it will be argued that there is evidence of potential benefits for victims in engaging with restorative justice initiatives.

Chapter Three having examined the implications of the community justice and restorative justice movements for victims, Chapter Four continues the comparative analysis in respect of other aspects of victim policy such as compensation, keeping victims informed about the progress of 'their' offenders' cases and direct service provision to victims. Some of the lessons which can be learnt from experience in a number of countries are discussed and mistakes which should not be repeated are identified.

Chapter Five focuses upon effective service provision for victims, again drawing upon examples from a number of jurisdictions. The need to listen to victims themselves is emphasised, and the benefits of policymakers and researchers involving participants in the criminal justice system and learning from their experience are illustrated.

Finally, Chapter Six offers some conclusions and discusses implications for the future, identifying an agenda for future research and some areas of policy and practice which are ripe for change. In particular, the current model of service provision is examined in the light of what we now know about corporate and organised crime: these involve large numbers of individual victims whose needs are not met effectively by existing policies or services.

Victim policy 1963–2004

How genuine is the apparent political interest in victims of crime?

It is easy for politicians to claim that they intend to 'do something' about the position of victims of crime. Over the years, a large number of such initiatives have been taken without necessarily resulting in much actual benefit for victims of crime. Such symbolic or rhetorical policymaking can be damaging. A few recent examples from the British Isles will suffice to illustrate the point.

The 1990 Victim's Charter (Home Office 1990) ostensibly codified victims' rights, but in law and practice it was clear that no new rights were created and the original charter was more of a wish-list than a 'statement of the rights of victims of crime' (to quote its original subtitle). The charter's subtitle was subsequently changed in the 1996 edition to reflect the reality more closely: it was re-named a 'statement of service standards for victims of crime'. However, the misleading impression created by the first edition called the motivation behind the whole enterprise into question, and was in danger of discrediting it. It eventually had to be replaced with legislation, but in the intervening 15 years it undoubtedly helped to raise expectations among victims of individual, interpersonal crime and their supporters (neglecting the victims of corporate crime). A similar approach to victims' rights was taken in Ireland, but the Irish *Victim's Charter and Guide to the Criminal Justice System* (DJELR 1999) provides victims with more information about the law and the criminal justice system. Although it is lengthier, it may prove more useful as a first step in driving change within the agencies involved. However, it comes some years after the first attempt at this approach in the UK and, like the UK charter, it is neither well-known nor well-publicised. It also creates no new rights, but rather lists the responses victims can reasonably expect from the relevant criminal justice agencies.

Victim Personal Statements were introduced in England and Wales in 2001 with the intention of giving victims an opportunity to express their concerns and describe the loss and damage they suffered to those in the criminal justice system with responsibility for making decisions about the offence and the offender. The scheme in England and Wales was meant to avoid the pitfalls of Victim Impact Statements in other jurisdictions. In practice these statements are routinely taken from victims but they rarely seem to leave police stations to fulfil their intended function of informing the decision-making of other criminal justice agencies in the light of victims' experiences. This has major implications for victims' confidence in the criminal justice system: their participation is solicited but their views are not actually taken into account because of administrative blockages or institutional resistance to change. From many victims' point of view, this is a sign of bad faith on the part of the criminal justice system, and many are likely to feel that it would have been better if they had never been consulted at all.

A less well-known example is the requirement (since 1995) for report writers in the probation service in England and Wales to address victim concerns in Pre-Sentence Reports which provide information for courts prior to the sentencing of offenders. While the aim was laudable, it proved very difficult to implement in many areas due to communication problems between the Crown Prosecution Service (CPS) and probation (Dominey 2002). Probation officers found themselves unable to reflect the impact of offences upon victims with any degree of accuracy because the CPS failed to give them the relevant information on which to base such assessments. This is an example of policy being made without the necessary steps being taken to ensure that it can be implemented in practice. This, too, calls the legislators' good faith into question in victims' eyes.

In some cases, the process goes even further. Not only are symbolic changes made which do not really benefit victims, they are made at the expense of other groups within the criminal justice system (in practice, princi-pally offenders). There is a fundamental misunderstanding here. First, victims and offenders are overlapping, rather than discrete, groups. Second, rights are not finite: it is not always necessary to reduce the rights of one party in a dispute in order to improve the position of another. Third, this approach – like rhetorical policymaking – neglects the potential psychological consequences for victims: 'Providing rights without remedies would result in the worst of consequences, such as feelings of helplessness, lack of control, and further vic-timization' (Kilpatrick and Otto 1987, cited in Davis, Henderson and Rabbitt 2002).

Examples of the consequences of this type of thinking include:

- The idiosyncratic decision, in England and Wales, to make Reparation Orders mandatory for young offenders while making victim participation voluntary: elsewhere reparation works perfectly well on the basis of voluntary participation by all parties (Umbreit 2001, p.27; Williams 2001; Johnstone 2002; but for a contrary view see Crawford and Newburn 2003, pp.47–8). Victims in a number of countries receive direct or symbolic recompense from young offenders without coercion. Not unnaturally, victims are more likely to experience satisfaction if they feel that the young person has undertaken reparation from genuine motives rather than merely because it is required by the court.

- Increased sentencing powers as a logical response to what Ashworth (2000, p.186) called the 'victims in the service of severity' thesis (see also Garland 2001). Examples include the so-called 'three strikes and you're out' provision of the UK's Crime [Sentences] Act 1997, which was based upon earlier, similar changes in the USA (see Cavadino and Dignan 2002). Under this approach, courts are encouraged to sentence offenders more severely – sometimes even to life imprisonment – in specific types of case in the name of protecting victims. Not only does this pandering to the revenge motive make matters no better for victims in general, it may mean the eventual release of embittered and vindictive offenders who feel with some justice that they have been punished disproportionately, which cannot be of any assistance to victims (see Chapter Four).

Aspects of the politicisation of victim issues are, therefore, severely counter-productive in terms of victims' real interests, and many of these changes were made without any consultation with victims or the organisations which represent their interests. Alongside changing attitudes towards victims at the national political level, the period since the 1970s has also seen the development of an influential victims' movement. The history of these two developments will now be traced, before further consideration is given the consequences of the politicisation of victims' issues.

Development of victim policy internationally since 1963

This chapter continues by outlining a brief history of victim policy internationally, which aims to show how certain common themes have dominated the history of this area of policy. It is far from comprehensive: the examples of compensation, state aid for victim support agencies, protection for victims and witnesses, arrangements for keeping victims informed and taking their views into account and the introduction of international standards for the treatment of victims are used to illustrate the development of victim policy. Most of these themes are revisited in greater detail in later chapters.

Compensation

Compensation to crime victims is an ancient tradition in many cultures (Black 1987). However, the year 1963 is chosen as the starting point for this brief review of the development of victim policy internationally because it has considerable symbolic importance in the development of criminal justice systems in modern times. It was in that year that the New Zealand government legislated for a compensation scheme for the victims of certain types of crime; this was followed in 1964 by the introduction of a similar scheme in the UK, initially on an experimental basis but later made statutory. Other countries followed suit over the coming decades (including Sweden, The Netherlands, Norway, Denmark and France in the 1970s and Luxembourg in 1984; for further detail, see Brienen and Hoegen 2000 and Howard League for Penal Reform, 1977). Some US states also introduced statutory compensation schemes over the same period, beginning with California in 1966. In many countries, the introduction of an official compensation scheme for victims of crime – usually limited to specific types of crime such as violent and sexual offences – has been the first legislative manifestation of concern about victims' needs. Setting up such arrangements shows official recognition not only of victims' needs but also of the responsibility of the state for contributing towards meeting these.

However, the compensation scheme as it exists in the UK does not symbolise any kind of official recognition of state liability for the injuries caused by crime. The White Paper which proposed the experimental scheme made this clear. Rather, it is a welfare payment (Meiners 1978). As the White Paper put it,

> Compensation will be paid *ex gratia*. The government does not accept that the state is liable for injuries caused to people by the acts of others. The public does, however, feel a sense of responsibility for…the innocent victim, and it is right that this feeling should find practical expression in the provision of compensation… (Home Office 1964, quoted in Meiners 1978, p.3)

The recognition of compensation as a responsibility of the welfare state took many years to achieve: in the UK, the Howard League for Penal Reform had advocated state-funded compensation and direct compensation by offenders to victims since at least 1900, and magistrate and social reformer Margery Fry spearheaded its campaign in the 1950s, influencing both the New Zealand and the UK legislation (see Fry 1951; Edelhertz and Geis 1974; Rock 1990). The organisation Justice joined the Howard League in its campaign for a compensation scheme in the 1950s and 1960s. Fry saw state compensation as a form of social insurance, arguing that 'the logical way of providing for criminally inflicted injuries would be to tax every adult citizen…to cover a risk to which each is exposed (Fry 1957, quoted in Edelhertz and Geis 1974, p.10).

Similarly, legal reforms were first proposed in The Netherlands in 1896, and these were framed in terms of the 'indemnification' of the victim of crime (Boutellier 2000). This 'social insurance' model was persuasive, encouraging governments to accept responsibility (but not legal liability) for compensating certain victims. As such, it represented an important change in official attitudes towards the victims of crime, recognising them for the first time as a group in need of support and meriting collective provision. However, there was undoubtedly also an element, at the time, of advocating a reform – any reform – which impacted upon victims because of the persistent tendency of those opposing penal reform to raise the question, 'What about the victim?', reflecting a widespread belief that too much attention was being paid at that time to the needs of offenders (see Rock 1990, Chapter Two).

The compensation scheme eventually proposed had clear limits upon eligibility, and the UK scheme was influential in its discrimination between 'deserving' and 'undeserving' victims, a distinction which remains a sore point to this day. State compensation in the UK explicitly excludes certain categories of victims defined as undeserving: the White Paper's emphasis upon 'innocent' victims is significant (and its implications are discussed in Chapter Four). Among the probable reasons for this was the failure at any stage during the campaign for state compensation to consult victims themselves about what they wanted. Another reason, perhaps, is the reformers' naivety about the sorts of people who become victims and the relationship between victim and offender statuses: victims and offenders are overlapping rather than discrete groups (Rock 1990, 2004; Walklate 2004).

Offenders themselves can also be required to pay compensation to victims, as a sentence of a criminal court. In many countries, victims have an additional right to take civil legal proceedings in an attempt to secure compensation, but this tends to be expensive and time-consuming, and it is not an option open to most victims even in rich countries such as the USA. Some victims are also able to claim on household insurance, but whether people have insurance similarly varies according to their income (Doerner and Lab 2002). This makes the acceptance of a case for some state provision all the more important.

Court-ordered compensation depends upon effective enforcement measures, and this has been a stumbling block in a number of countries (see Chapter Four). Governments have concerned themselves with the principles of compensation by offenders to victims, but in the UK the issue has had to be revisited regularly in Parliament because of problems in enforcement: victims' expectations of receiving payment may be raised by the making of an award against the offender, but subsequently dashed by the failure to collect and pass on the money. The 1988 Criminal Justice Act, under which courts in England and Wales were required to give reasons for not ordering compensation in all relevant cases, would have been a constructive change from victims' point of view had it been consistently implemented. It was not, however, and in many courts compensation was not routinely awarded to victims who might have qualified for it, not least because the prosecution service failed to pass on the information the courts required in order to facilitate this process. It is unhelpful for laws relating to victims to be passed and not consistently implemented, as with this legislation, because it can adversely affect victims' confidence in the criminal justice system, already low in many cases. Victims' expectations are raised but not fulfilled, which can produce cynicism and contribute to questions being raised about the legitimacy and justice of the system.

State aid for victim support agencies

In many countries, the impetus for state interest in issues concerning victims has come from non-governmental organisations set up to provide services to individual victims or to campaign for improvements in their treatment by official agencies (or both). In the UK, the growth of the women's refuge movement in the early 1970s, followed by Victim Support and rape crisis centres later in the same decade, provided examples of practical needs which were going unmet as well as creating a network of agencies capable of meeting these needs and a growing group of well-informed advocates for victims. All three initiatives replicated the emergence of similar voluntary agencies in North America from the 1960s onwards. In the USA, however, the establishment of these service agencies was accompanied by the growth of local and national victims' advocacy groups dedicated to campaigning activities (including 'court watcher' programmes which highlighted allegedly lenient sentences, and the campaigns for a Federal compensation programme for victims and for the introduction of victim impact statements: see Mawby and Gill 1987). Many of these organisations worked independently of service provider groups, until the two wings of the emergent victims' movement came together for some purposes in an informal coalition under the umbrella organisation NOVA (the National Organization for Victim Assistance) in the early 1970s. Other groups, however, consistently combined victim assistance with campaigning activity, as in the case of Mothers Against Drunk Driving (formed in California in 1980).

The extent to which victim organisations formulate and promote a political analysis of the issues around victimisation clearly influences the extent to which they can draw upon state financial support for their work. This is, however, a complex dynamic. In North America, for example, some campaign groups have explicitly or implicitly espoused right-wing politics, while others were feminist-inspired and yet others were part of a wider campaign for greater state expenditure on welfare programmes. Overall, in the USA, the victims' movement could be characterised as concerned primarily with victims' rights, including the right to receive professional counselling (Mawby and Gill 1987; Mawby 2003). In the UK, there is a greater tradition of voluntarism and (although it is not the only reason) the legal restriction on political campaigning by charitable organisations has restrained victim groups from explicit involvement in politics. Indeed, a number of observers have argued that Victim Support in the UK has steered a carefully apolitical course from its earliest days. In the beginning, there was a perceived need to distance itself from radical groups which were vocally critical of the police (Rock 1990, p.165). It was organised in a highly centralised way so that information (and funding) came from the centre and local dissent could easily be suppressed. Once these structures were established, the Home Office invited the organisation to apply for government funding towards the cost of its work (Rock 1990, p.168), which could be seen as deliberate co-option and incorporation, or as recognition of its achievements and campaigns. In practice, both are to some extent true.

In the USA, victims' organisations have become involved in political campaigning partly in order to gain access to Federal funding, whereas in the UK their restraint and reticence about making political pronouncements have traditionally made it more likely that they will receive some state funding as well as financial support from charitable trusts (Rock 1990).

US victim support programmes operate mainly at the state rather than the Federal level, and mostly receive their funding indirectly from offenders (from fines, from the seizure of criminally obtained assets and from mandatory surcharges levied upon convicted offenders for the purpose: see Doerner and Lab 2002). Indirect funding for victim support agencies from offenders has been introduced in the UK as part of the Domestic Violence, Crime and Victims Act 2004, but it has been controversial and the proposals were amended in response to media and other criticism to remove most types of motoring offenders from its scope (Home Office 2004c; BBC News 2004; Hansard 2004: see also Chapter Four).

In England and Wales, annual state funding for Victim Support increased from £5000 when it was first granted in 1979 to £17 million 20 years later (Zedner 2002) and to £29 million by 2002/03 (Victim Support 2004b). After a further increase to over £30 million the following year, the Home Office indicated that 'the likelihood of extra resources is slim' in the coming years (Potter 2004, p.11), despite the additional income expected from the surcharges on fines and fixed penalty payments from 2005.

Elsewhere, the next experimental victim support schemes were first set up (by the probation service) in The Netherlands in 1975, and an independent national organisation was established in 1984. State funding was received from national and local government departments for the cost of employing a network of staff but, as in the UK, the main contact with victims is delivered by volunteers. Some Dutch schemes are independent, while others are provided by local welfare or police departments (Mawby 2003).

National organisations were also set up in the 1980s in France and Germany. In Germany there are in fact two organisations: the Weisser Ring, which covers the whole country, complemented by additional local services for the town of Hanau. The latter are funded by local government, while the Weisser Ring is a voluntary organisation which receives payments from the fund which collects court fines from offenders. It delivers some direct victim support but is primarily a campaigning organisation (Mawby 2003). In France INAVEM, the National Institute for the Assistance of Victims, serves as a co-ordinating body promoting best practice and preparing national standards, for local services which concentrate primarily upon legal advice, mediation and practical assistance rather than emotional support (although this is perhaps an artificial distinction in this context). NOVS serves similar functions in The Netherlands (Mawby and Walklate 1994). Victim–offender mediation is provided in a number of countries using volunteers or sessional staff paid a nominal fee (see Chapter Three) and it seems that there are ideological reasons for the differences in the extent to which this kind of provision is seen as a statutory or a voluntary sector responsibility. It is clear from the above, however, that in many wealthy countries, victim support agencies are well-established and supported both by the state and by the commitment of large numbers of volunteers.

Protection for victims and witnesses in three countries

Increased awareness of the needs of victims of crime has been manifested in a number of countries in the form of improvements in the arrangements for the protection of victims and witnesses, both pre-trial and at court. In the UK, a series of reforms was introduced to make the experience of giving evidence in cases of rape and sexual assault less traumatic, beginning with the introduction of some protection of the identities and addresses of complainants in 1976 legislation. Video links were introduced in child abuse cases in 1988 and in sexual offence cases in 1999.

In the USA, Federal legislation in 1982 introduced specific penalties for interfering with witnesses, and similar provisions apply in the UK (both in relation to the revocation of bail (Home Office 2000) and under legislation on intimidating or taking revenge against witnesses.[1] In addition, the police in most countries offer a graduated response to witnesses depending on an assessment of their needs and vulnerabilities. This tends to be a more sophisticated process in densely populated urban areas, some of which, in England and Wales and in Scotland, have specialist witness care departments either within the police or as part of multi-agency collaborations. National government has funded pilot projects in several areas which bring together representatives of all the agencies that work with victims and witnesses to provide an integrated support service. This has led to improved rates of attendance at court by witnesses, increased referral rates to Victim Support and the Witness Service, greater take-up of Victim Personal Statements and a better police service to victims, according to an interim evaluation by project staff in the Warwickshire Victim and Witness Information Partnership and interim findings of the research on the other pilot projects (govnet 2004). The success of these projects, along with the responses to a public consultation exercise, persuaded the government that increased support for witnesses, rather than punishment of those who failed to attend court, was the best way forward. As a result, dedicated witness care units were established throughout the country in 2004/05, providing a range of support including assistance with transport and child-care in appropriate cases. In most parts of the country, additionally, there is provision for physical protection from intimidation, the appointment of named individuals as liaison officers in more serious cases, police escorts to and from court, and so on (Williams 2002). In theory, it has been possible for courts in England and Wales to accept written statements by intimidated witnesses since 1988, but this power was rarely used (see McEwan 2002).

A specialist family violence court was set up in one city, Winnipeg in Canada, in 1990 with a view to developing specialist expertise on the part of sentencers, speeding up sentencing, delivering appropriate programmes for offenders and protecting the victims in 'domestic' violence cases. It succeeded in increasing rates of reporting by victims and the conviction rates. Perhaps surprisingly, the increased convictions resulted in a greater use of community rather than custodial sentences for offenders: the court favoured probation with a condition of attendance at a group work programme (Ursel 2002). This experiment has been replicated elsewhere in Canada and in a number of other countries, including the USA and Scotland. In addition to the benefits already

---

1   The relevant legislation is the Criminal Justice and Public Order Act 1994: see also HSE (undated).

mentioned, an advantage of this approach from victims' point of view is the reduction of courts' reliance upon the testimony of victims themselves: alternative types of evidence are found, and prosecutions can proceed even without victims' co-operation. The court has also collaborated with the probation service to ensure the availability of community programmes for perpetrators which avoid the necessity of imprisoning offenders, at least in less serious cases – recognising that immediate imprisonment is not usually welcomed by victims and their families (see Chapter Five).

However, research in the specialist court in Toronto has found that the combination of mandatory arrest policies and the introduction of the specialised court has not changed prosecutors' preference for 'co-operative' victims: cases are still seven times as likely to proceed to prosecution if the prosecutor perceives the victim to be co-operative (Dawson and Dinovitzer 2001). The same research also found that victims were more likely to co-operate if two conditions were met: they were more inclined to do so in cases where the police had collected evidence at the outset which reduced the necessity for victims to give oral testimony in court (particularly videotaped statements and photographs of the victims' injuries), and also in cases where they received support from the Victim/Witness Assistance Program attached to the court. This service contacts victims proactively in order to provide support, information about the legal process, referrals to other agencies, and someone to accompany them both to court and to any meetings with the prosecution. The researchers suggest that these factors are likely to be equally applicable elsewhere, and that changes in police training and practice and the provision of appropriate support to victims will lead to fuller co-operation and more successful prosecutions wherever these are put into place.

A US judge has argued that sentencers in specialist courts gain greater experience in dealing with domestic violence cases than judges would typically have, and they are better able to maintain oversight of the offenders they sentence, ensuring compliance with court orders or, at least, effective sanctions when these are breached. In turn, it has been argued that 'the court's focus on domestic violence emphasizes to the community both the seriousness of domestic violence and the dedication of the justice system to addressing the problem' (Karan, Keilitz and Denaro 1999, p.76).

Such a court is often in a position to bring together complex issues concerning domestic violence and violence against children, and sometimes also divorce cases, to consider them in a holistic manner. This may prevent further serious violence – and even murders – in some cases (see Karan *et al.* 1999 for case studies).

A wider view of victims' and witnesses' need for protection was taken in the UK with the introduction of legislation in 1999 which defined all young people under the age of 17 appearing in court, and a range of other categories of people, as 'vulnerable witnesses' and specified a range of types of assistance this status entitled them to receive. The categories of witnesses covered include people with reasonable fears about giving evidence, those likely to be particularly distressed by the experience of doing so and people with a range of mental and physical disabilities and communication difficulties. All complainants in sexual offence cases are also normally covered by the legal notion of vulnerability. Once the court has established that the legislation applies in a particular case, the 'special measures' available include the use of intermediaries to assist witnesses' communication with the court, the use of screens to prevent witnesses and defendants from seeing one another in court, the use of video links so that witnesses do not have to be present in the court room at all, the exclusion of the press in certain cases and the removal of lawyers' wigs and gowns in order to avoid unnecessary formality. There is also a rule against the defendant who is unrepresented cross-examining witnesses in sexual offences trials. This list of special measures gives courts considerable flexibility in responding to the needs of particular witnesses: in each case, the law requires that special measures be made available if the court is of the opinion that this would 'be likely to improve the quality of evidence given by the witness' (Youth Justice and Criminal Evidence Act 1999, s. 19 (2) (a)).

While this might seem a somewhat instrumental approach to making special provisions available, it opens the door to a wide range of assistance for witnesses. Indeed, some have argued that it goes too far and prejudices the rights of defendants. If there are vulnerable witnesses, are there not also vulnerable defendants who should be entitled to similar protections (Spencer 2004)? However, another academic lawyer has convincingly argued that the special measures go nowhere near far enough in terms of protecting victims from intrusive and intimidating questioning in court (Ellison 2001). She argues that the British legal profession's obsession with testing evidence orally in front of an audience has inhibited efforts to improve witnesses' ability to give their best evidence. This is discussed further in Chapter Six.

Recognising how stressful it can be to give evidence in criminal cases, Victim Support in the UK experimented with the provision of targeted support to witnesses. By 1996 there was a national network of such schemes in the higher courts, and this was subsequently replicated in magistrates' courts. Witness Support, as the sister organisation of Victim Support became known, supervises separate waiting areas for witnesses, provides informal support from trained volunteers before and after witnesses' cases are heard and sets up opportunities for witnesses to visit the court before the case and familiarise themselves with the physical layout and court procedures. The projects also liaise with court administrators about general issues affecting the interests of witnesses (see Chapter Five for a fuller discussion).

Keeping victims informed and taking their views into account

The research literature consistently shows that one of the main grievances victims express about their treatment by the criminal justice system is the failure to keep them informed (see, for example, Shapland, Willmore and Duff 1985; Newburn and Merry, 1990; Macpherson, 1999; Maguire and Kynch, 2000; Curry *et al.* 2004). Much of the research has focused upon the failings of the police, probably because most victims see them as the natural point of contact with the system, but consumer research in other criminal justice agencies has provided evidence of similar discontent.

In the case of the courts, Victim Support in the UK has responded to evidence that victims found courts forbidding places where it was unclear to whom they should report, how they might behave and from whom they should seek protection in cases of intimidation, by establishing Witness Support projects (briefly described in the previous section). Elsewhere, as in parts of the USA, victims' contact with criminal courts is still characterised by confusion and bewilderment because of the lack of such support services (Doerner and Lab 2002, p.60).

Prosecution services have traditionally distanced themselves from victims in the name of judicial independence, and this has tended to be used as a reason for not passing information on to them (Shapland and Bell 1998). While it is possible to impose statutory duties upon prosecutors, this does not necessarily result in the kind of cultural changes required to make prosecution lawyers more open to the needs of victims and witnesses. In a recent experiment in England and Wales, prosecutors have become involved in the decision about what offences to charge defendants with at an earlier stage, which at least makes it less likely that the police will tell a victim one thing, only to be contradicted by a prosecution service lawyer a few weeks later when the case is reviewed from a legal point of view. In many cases, this would involve a downgrading of the seriousness of the offence to be prosecuted, which is often seen as an unhelpful raising and then deflation of victims' expectations (Clark 2004). Changes have also been made to encourage prosecutors to inform victims about significant decisions, and to train them in doing this sensitively – but the issue appears to be one of how to change professional culture, which is unlikely to be solved merely by changing rules of conduct (Jackson 2004).

International standards for the treatment of victims

The right to be kept informed was enshrined in the first United Nations policy document on victims, along with fair treatment (including access to legal procedures), proper consideration of their views, restitution and compensation and the right to be provided with appropriate services (Sanders 1999; Zedner 2002). The UN *Declaration of the Basic Principles of Justice for Victims of Crime and Abuse of Power* used, as its name suggests, a broad definition of victims (United Nations 1985). In practice, this may have diluted its effectiveness in the criminal justice context, although it was intended to bring to international attention such emerging international issues of 'white collar' crime as the trafficking of women and children. Its standards have been described by an academic lawyer as 'vague and minimal' (Sanders 2002, p.202) and it seems to have represented a compromise between the differing views of those who drafted it, some of whom wanted a much stronger statement, but the publication of the declaration was something of a landmark nonetheless. As Sanders himself says, it formed the foundation for subsequent more specific recommendations and made it easier to argue for EU policies which are binding upon member states.

The momentum behind the preparation of the 1985 declaration came from a number of disparate quarters. The women's movement certainly played a part in raising awareness of the suffering and revictimisation by state agencies of women victims of sexual offences and male violence; the World Society of Victimology or WSV (which brought together academics and practitioners interested in the victims of crime) explicitly sought to influence UN policy and activities; and the UN's own agencies drew attention to the need to give greater priority to victim issues (Mawby and Walklate 1994). In particular, the Crime Prevention and Criminal Justice Branch of the UN's Economic and Social Council began to look at victim-related issues in 1975, and the WSV exerted pressure to keep up this momentum, culminating in the 1985 declaration.

Although, for many years, little follow-up action was taken by the UN in relation to the implementation of the 1985 declaration, a handbook for member states was eventually published in 1999 (United Nations 1999), accompanied by a brief guide for policymakers. These documents provide detailed guidance on how to develop victim-sensitive policies and services, building upon the experiences of countries which have established the effectiveness of particular approaches and covering the potential roles of a wide range of professionals as well as government and 'civil society' (in this context, referring primarily to non-governmental organisations) in assisting victims.

The European Union followed this up shortly afterwards with a Framework Decision by the Council of Ministers in 2001 on the standing of victims in criminal proceedings which was not only binding upon member countries from 2002, but also had provisions that must be satisfied by aspiring EU members as part of the accession process (Sanders 2002). It requires that member countries' legal systems treat victims with respect for their dignity, privacy and safety; ensure that it is possible for them to give evidence and 'be heard during proceedings' (article 3, European Union Council of Justice and Home Affairs 2001) and make provision for protection, support and information to be given to them – but states are left with 'considerable discretion' about detailed implementation (Dignan 2005, p.66). Although countries such as the UK, Ireland and Austria had to do little to comply with this directive, it had profound implications for the legal systems of other countries such as those joining the European Union (EU) in 2004 and those behind them in the queue. Thus, for example, experimental projects have been set up in countries such as Russia and Serbia partly inspired by the Framework Decision. This issue will be discussed further in Chapters Three and Four.

European court cases arising from the European Convention on Human Rights and other instruments have also expanded and clarified victims' rights in member states, for example in the area of witness protection (see Goodey 2005, pp.174–8).

Politicisation and the growth of the victims' movement

Despite the studied political neutrality of Victim Support in the UK for much of its existence, it has played its part in the politicisation of policy on victims of crime. For example, it was Victim Support which published an influential document listing the rights which, it argued, should be accorded to victims, at around the same time as it made public its opposition to the first of a number of central government interventions designed to curtail the criminal injuries compensation arrangements because of their increasing cost (Victim Support 1995; Williams 1999a, p.71). These issues became part of the debate about law and order in the general election just over a year later, and helped to provide the new government with a distinctive political agenda in the area of crime control. Most of the changes advocated in the 1995 document were, indeed, at least partially implemented by that government in the period

1997–2004, and they also influenced the EU Framework Decision on the Standing of Victims in Criminal Procedure (Rock 2004). Indeed, the relevant minister went so far as to argue that her government's 2004 Domestic Violence, Crime and Victims Act represented a near-complete implementation of Victim Support's 'wish list' (Potter 2004, p.12). Interestingly, though, the same government also returned to the issue of state compensation, making a further attempt to cut the cost of the scheme in 2004 (see Chapter Four).

Victim Support's 1995 paper had been augmented by a more explicitly political manifesto prior to the 2001 general election (Victim Support 2001), calling for the introduction of an ombudsman for victims as well as the implementation of the 1995 recommendations, and this was followed by more general policy demands in 2002 and 2004. The first of these pointed out how few victims of crime came to official notice, and argued that counselling, psychiatric and other health services, as well as housing and benefits where appropriate, should be available to all victims regardless of whether offences had been processed by the criminal justice system (Victim Support 2002). The second reiterated these arguments, pointing out the need for collaboration between agencies and greater awareness within them about meeting victims' needs, as well as setting out new areas of work which Victim Support wishes to pursue if and when further funding became available. Significantly, it also adopted the government's argument about the need to 'restore the balance in favour of victims' within the criminal justice system (Victim Support 2004a, p.15).

Victims were increasingly being characterised in policy debates as users, or even as *clients* or *consumers*, of the criminal justice system, although a number of observers have argued that this is a false analogy: victims have little choice about using criminal justice services and most would prefer not to be in the position of having to do so. They are reluctant clients at best, and they have very little choice as consumers (Williams 1999a; Zaubermann 2000; Rock 2004). This consumerist approach was part of a more general move towards encouraging communities to take greater responsibilities for crime and its aftermath at a local level, and of devolution of certain central state powers in the area of criminal justice (Walklate 2004). The 'service standards' or citizen's charter approach created new expectations among victims of crime, and the Victim's Charter made it clear that any dissatisfaction should be addressed to local service providers, despite the fact that these are funded and regulated by central government (Williams 1999b).

Elsewhere, similar dynamics can be observed. The growth of organisations representing victims (or claiming to do so) has led to successful demands for political change in a number of jurisdictions. In some countries, victims' organisations have been a good deal less inhibited about demanding political changes than those in the UK, although it is debateable to what extent some of the changes achieved have been in victims' real interests. To take an extreme example, in some states in the USA, victims have gained an entitlement to attend state executions of offenders as part of their quest for emotional 'closure'. Is this something that victims themselves campaigned for, or was it the result of a politically motivated campaign?

Around the world, organisations claiming to represent victims have become increasingly vocal and influential over the past thirty years, and in the process the issues involved have inevitably been politicised. This has both advantages and drawbacks in terms of its effects upon the treatment of victims of crime. On the one hand, services have undoubtedly improved as a result of this pressure in a variety of ways. On the other hand, though, politicians are apt to choose 'quick fix' solutions which do not necessarily improve victims' position (Walklate 2004).

What once appeared to be radical claims made by victimologists and feminists relating to the tendency of the criminal justice system to revictimise victims and witnesses, are now generally accepted facts. To this extent, the process of politicisation has undoubtedly been beneficial, in that the relevant agencies have been forced to address some deficiencies in the light of victims' experience and feedback (Goodey 2005). The danger which is sometimes hidden alongside these beneficial consequences of political awareness is that victim concerns become hijacked or co-opted by particular political constituencies, which is what many observers believe has happened in the USA and can happen elsewhere. In the process, victims' expressed wishes and needs can be overlooked or deliberately ignored.

Another danger is that splits occur between victim support agencies which prefer to work quietly within the system and those committed to exposing injustice in more public and often more politically combative ways. Such divisions can be exploited by politicians for a variety of reasons, and this may not result in improved policies or services (see Williams 1999; Goodey 2005).

The remainder of this book examines these processes in a number of countries, often drawing upon case material. Initially, a thematic approach is taken, looking first at community and then restorative justice, and their impact upon victims (Chapters Two and Three). In later chapters, more use is made of a comparative approach, looking first at the failures and then at the successes of a range of innovations in policy and practice relating to victims.

Chapter Two

Community justice and its implications for victims

The communitarian view of the solution to social problems urges policy-makers to strengthen the family and the other institutions which build up into healthy communities. It sees individuals as mutually interdependent and as having 'responsibilities towards a common good, at least as much as rights' (Nellis 2000, p.77). When it is applied to criminal justice settings, communitarian philosophy tends to promote what have become known as *community justice* approaches. These are important for victims of crime because of the claims that are made about the possible benefits of this reorientation of the justice system for victims, among others. In this chapter, these claims will be examined in the light of a number of examples of the implementation of community justice. Community justice will be distinguished from restorative justice (which is discussed in the next chapter) and some conclusions will be drawn about the actual and potential benefits of community justice for the victims of crime. The discussion will begin with community justice in North America, where it has established a firm foothold, going on to consider parallel developments in other parts of the world and their implications in terms of policy and practice concerning victims. It is worth noting that 'community justice' is a contested and ambiguous term, as will become apparent later in this chapter.

The development of community justice

Advocates of community justice argue that the criminal justice system should pay more attention to crime prevention. Community justice should be locally based, flexible and informal, and serve victims, communities, offenders and their families better than existing systems. It should provide opportunities for 'stakeholder participation', encompassing both individual involvement in the justice process and partnership with community agencies. It encourages take-up of criminal justice services such as mediation, through outreach work and by involving community members in managing and providing services (Altschuler 2001). In the process, it can become part of a process of 'community building', helping communities to develop their own 'social capital' and build creatively on the otherwise potentially destructive tensions caused by crime (Etzioni 1998, p.375). Its other prominent contemporary proponents in the USA, David Karp and Todd Clear argue that it has 'four central dimensions: system accessibility, citizen involvement, restorative justice, and offender reintegration' (Karp and Clear 2002, p.xiii).

The inclusion of restorative justice (RJ) in this list of characteristics of community justice is problematic in many people's eyes, subsuming RJ as but one characteristic of community justice when it can be seen as a new paradigm in its own right. This issue is discussed further below.

The extent to which greater democratic participation in criminal justice should be encouraged depends upon the legitimacy and fairness of the system, and it may be risky to encourage citizen participation in an unequal system which lacks public confidence: 'it is dangerous to open up criminal justice issues to democratic participation at precisely the moment when trust between groups of citizens, and between citizens and government, is weakest' (Jordan and Arnold 1995, p.180).

Nevertheless, the context for the rise of community justice is a loss of confidence in existing methods of managing offenders within the community (particularly in the USA), along with an explosion in the use of imprisonment. There is, on the other hand, increasing disenchantment with the 'adversarial, war-on-crime model' of criminal justice and an increasingly frantic search for more constructive alternatives (Clear and Karp 1998, p.9). However, the idea of community justice is not as new as its current advocates sometimes claim:

> Since the 1960s we have seen the development of one community programme after another – community corrections, community policing, punishment in the community, community crime prevention, community prosecution, community justice. 'The community' has become the all-purpose solution to every criminal justice problem. (Garland 2001, p.123)

In policing as well as in probation and youth justice, these ideas have been advocated both in North America and in Europe since at least the 1960s, although they have gone in and out of fashion during that period. Garland argues that they now form part of a 'responsibilization strategy' by central governments, aimed at shifting responsibility for the management of crime at least partly away from the state and encouraging local communities to share the responsibility for managing crime and its consequences. He points out that this shift is often characterised by a move towards inter-agency partnership and partnerships between the state and the private and voluntary sectors. One consequence is the proliferation of organisations such as community safety partnerships and referral order panels (to give just two examples from England and Wales) which make new demands upon local communities, including victim support agencies. This is discussed later in this chapter.

Often linked to the notion of responsibilisation is communitarian writers' hankering after the recreation of an idealised version of small-town American values, civic virtues and moral consensus (Hughes 2001b). While this ideal past may be mythical, it has created a focus for the campaign for community justice in America; it has also undoubtedly influenced political discourse and decisions in the UK, particularly in the period since the mid-1990s (Nellis 2000). While there are questions about how inclusive, and how practicable, such models of community justice are likely to be in fragmented inner-city areas, there are those who suggest that the model is as persuasive in such environments as in rural and suburban communities. Demoralised areas can benefit from the creation and restoration of social capital involved in community justice initiatives, they argue (see for example Braithwaite and Daly 1994; Faulkner 1994; Nellis 2000; and, from a more critical standpoint, Hughes 2000).

Communitarianism has two distinct strands, an authoritarian one and a more inclusive one. Both extremes are clearly visible in political pronouncements and decisions in the criminal justice sphere in the UK, many of which draw upon the US experience. Community justice has been characterised as a way of involving a wider constituency in the administration of justice and encouraging communities to take greater responsibility for the management of disorder rather than expelling offenders to remote institutions. It arises inevitably from the shift away from a welfare state in which state provision dominated (the state did the rowing, but it took little part in steering civil society), towards a 'new regulatory state' in which the state steers and civil society takes over the rowing (Etzioni 1994; Braithwaite 2000). National UK crime policy, it might be argued, reflected this in the mantra 'tough on crime and tough on the causes of crime' and in the creation of new structures such as inter-agency youth offending teams and drug action teams. Alternatively (and simultaneously) it has been seen as part of the drift towards centralisation and managerialism, with increasing emphasis upon the effectiveness, efficiency and economy of services and greater central scrutiny of the process of 'modernisation', alongside greater use of imprisonment and other forms of incarceration (McLaughlin and Muncie 2000; Nellis 2000). Far from returning services to local communities or civil society, these trends tend to make them more remote and depersonalised, as for example in the programme of closure of small local courts and their replacement by relatively remote and inaccessible but more modern, centralised facilities in England in the late 1990s.

While Saul Alinsky (1972) and his contemporaries were developing the idea of community justice in the USA, similar thinking was going on in northern Europe. Nils Christie's ideas were becoming widely known as a result of his influential article on 'conflicts as property' (Christie 1977), in which he argued that conflicts between people present opportunities which are appropriated by state agencies rather than being *used* by the parties directly involved, who are the experts on their own situation, to improve their relationships. He characterised the formal justice system as remote, hidden from public view, forbidding, impersonal, alienating, awe-inspiring, frightening and unnecessarily mystified by baffling jargon. The conflicts acted out in courts appear to belong to the lawyers, not to the parties involved, and esoteric rules determine what information is and is not regarded as relevant to a case. Victims – and offenders – are marginalised. This is a description of lived experiences of criminal justice which is recognisable today, and which one hears in the indignant accounts of the experiences of first-time parties attending court, whether as witnesses or defendants. Christie argued, instead, for a 'victim-oriented court' which mobilised community resources to help meet the needs of victims and offenders where required and for a 'lay-oriented court' which relied less heavily upon professional 'experts':

> it ought to be a court of equals representing themselves. When they are able to find a solution between themselves, no judges are needed. When they are not, the judges ought also to be their equals… Experts are as cancer to any lay body. (Christie 2004, p.28)

While he acknowledged the considerable obstacles in the way of implementing a new system based upon his vision, Christie's ideas nevertheless inspired much pressure for change within the system, not least in the area of victim involvement and services for victims in criminal justice. His article and his subsequent work have frequently been cited as part of the argument for individualised, accessible, comprehensible, empowering local services to victims delivered in ways which are congenial to and fully involve services' users (see for example Zehr 1990; Mawby and Walklate 1994; Umbreit 2001; Braithwaite 2002; Johnstone 2002).

Defining community justice

It is clear from the discussion in the previous section that there is a lack of consensus about exactly what 'community justice' means, and this has contributed to confusion in the discussion of the merits of introducing it internationally (Nellis 2000; Altschuler 2001; Faulkner 2001). It means different things to different people, as so often in political discourse: the concept has been redefined in use, and used to package a variety of approaches to problems. In some cases, the idea of community justice has been appropriated in an attempt to re-launch jaded programmes, or to justify off-loading central government responsibilities (Hughes 2001b). This will become obvious when examples of its practical implementation are described in the section that follows. Not surprisingly, it is difficult to offer a succinct definition. However, there appears to be widespread agreement on a number of issues, and considering these makes it easier to contemplate the possibility of defining the meaning of the term.

The very use of the term 'community justice' signifies approval of the principle of involving members of the local community in some aspect of criminal justice, in a range of capacities such as volunteers, lay (that is, non-professional) sentencers, mentors, panel members, supporters of victims or offenders, and mediators. Such involvement is seen as more inclusive than existing approaches, and thus as more representative and more likely to be 'owned' by the communities concerned. It is also welcomed as a step towards a less professionalised system, which it is hoped will be less alienating and more accessible.

Informal dispute resolution tends to be seen as more practical and more satisfying for the participants than professionalised approaches. As Christie argued, the formal system appropriates conflicts, whereas informal methods can resolve them within the community and allow participants to retain ownership of the process and to feel committed to the outcome.

Community justice implies a preference for solutions at the neighbour-hood level and a rejection of remote, bureaucratised approaches which are dominated by statutory agencies such as the police, prosecution or proba-tion services.

Community justice emphasises the potential for crime control to take place 'in the community' rather than in institutional settings, and it draws upon critiques of total institutions such as the prison and the secure training centre for young offenders, upon arguments about the dangers of stigma and exclusion and upon 'a belief in the healing powers of community rela-tions' (Garland 2001, p. 123).

Rather than being delivered by monolithic state agencies, community justice is often seen as necessitating enhanced partnerships between these criminal justice agencies and non-statutory organisations such as victim support agencies. It also generally requires improved arrangements for co-operation between the various statutory agencies and greater openness by these bodies to information sharing and community consultation.

Some advocates of community justice also argue for a 'mixed economy' of informal social control, involving a wider constituency of participant organisations such as residents' groups, local businesses, faith groups and others who would not conventionally be seen as part of crime or overt social control arrangements (this is arguably part of the strategy of 'respon-sibilisation' discussed above). The mixed economy may also imply a role in the delivery of local justice for commercial providers of social control services such as private security companies and those providing surveillance technologies.

Broadly, then, community justice is usually more representative of the com-munity and less professionalised than conventional criminal justice, although in some versions it involves commercial companies to a certain extent. Because it involves local people and organisations in decision-making and service delivery, it is more likely to be owned and seen as legitimate by com-munity members. It favours solving problems and resolving disputes at the local level, rejecting institutionalisation and bureaucratic modes of organisa-tion, and is thus more inclusive than the traditional system. It promotes co-operation between state and voluntary agencies and the involvement of local stakeholders. At its best it also encourages better liaison between statu-tory agencies themselves, and between them and community groups. It is attractive to central government both because of its potential for increasing the perceived legitimacy of criminal justice (and enhancing citizens' involvement in democratic institutions) and for its relatively low cost as compared to traditional measures such as incarceration – but sometimes also because of the potential for injecting a further commercial element into the criminal justice system.

Community justice in practice

There is clearly a need for checks and balances in any system of community justice: just like the system it seeks to modify or replace, it has to achieve legitimacy in the eyes of participants and the wider public, and to do so it has to dispense justice impartially, proportionally and with fairness and accountability. Informal justice can be a contradiction in terms, leading to arbitrary decision-making, domination by particular interest groups or even vigilantism (Faulkner 2001). One of the standards by which experiments in community justice must be judged is the extent to which they conform to these requirements.

They will also be judged by the extent to which they live up to their own aspirations: the definition of community justice given above is a tall order to put into practice. It also avoids some of the more controversial issues discussed earlier: there is an uneasy coalition of forces supporting the idea of community justice, certainly in the USA, and this has become apparent as some of the experimental projects have been exposed to wider scrutiny. Some of what has been done in the name of community justice is considerably more authoritarian than the system it seeks to replace, which is disturbing given its proponents' arguments about its democratic potential. As Altschuler (2001, p.29) has noted, the more conservative definition of community justice has 'at least to this point...prevailed over the liberal approach' in the USA.

The centrality of victims of crime is arguably also a yardstick of the success of a change towards a community justice approach, although victims are not always discussed in any depth in many of the descriptions of community justice projects or in the more abstract literature about the virtues of such an approach. Victims represent their communities just as much as offenders do, and community justice initiatives do not necessarily reflect this fully.

The remainder of this chapter aims to describe, briefly, some of the ways in which community justice has been put into practice in the USA and elsewhere, before considering some of the issues raised by these experimental approaches. It is worth noting that the terminology has become institutionalised to a far greater extent in Canada and the USA, where community justice centres and departments of community justice are common, than in other

English-speaking countries. In Australia, South Africa and the UK the phrase is more commonly attached to academic courses for criminal justice staff and to discussion forums such as the Community Justice Portal (http://www.cjp.org.uk) and the *British Journal of Community Justice.*

Comparing widely differing societies is fraught with difficulties and the lessons from community justice experiments in the USA will, inevitably, only have limited relevance in other jurisdictions. For example, as Christie (2000, p.168) reminds us, the USA has elected judges, but 'in the realities of modern societies, to be democratically elected does not mean representing everybody'. Elected judges are likely to be sensitive to community opinion in different ways to lay magistrates in the UK or professional judges in Italy or other countries with a separate judicial profession – and this is only one of the differences between those jurisdictions. It is therefore important to make comparisons very cautiously.

Community reparative boards in Vermont, USA

In the early 1990s, the predominantly rural US state of Vermont polled its residents about crime and justice. This exercise arose from concern about prison overcrowding and the soaring cost of providing prison places (Osborne and Plastrick 2000), and to this extent the initiative might be described as offender-led (see Chapter Three). As a result of this consultation exercise, considerable support was expressed for greater citizen involvement in decision-making about individual non-violent offenders. Voters were invited to express a view about a specific proposal, to establish community reparations boards, and 92 per cent of respondents supported the idea. From 1995, this was implemented, in modified form, in relation to minor non-violent offences. The initiative was renamed as 'community reparative boards' and these were evaluated by David Karp and his colleagues (Karp 2002). That research, which included videotapes of board meetings transcribed for the report, provides a valuable insight into the ways in which the idea was put into practice.

Offenders initially appear in court, and taking part in a board meeting is made a condition of probation in those cases assessed as suitable where the offender consents. Staff conduct intake interviews and schedule board meetings; they also take responsibility for mobilising appropriate resources, inviting the parties to the meeting, and monitoring offenders' compliance with agreed conditions. Few serious offenders are referred, although the courts have discretion to do so. Somewhere between three and five local volunteers constitute each meeting of a board. Initially recruited from among 'prominent local leaders', boards are now seeking to become more representative of the communities they serve. Members undergo 15 hours of training and observe meetings before beginning to take a full part, and ongoing training is also provided.

At the meeting, panel members begin by introducing themselves and reminding themselves of the contents of the documentation about the offence. The offender is invited to describe the offence and say something about him- or herself. Often, panel members will then ask the offender to leave while they have a private discussion. The agreement is then negotiated, taking into account any information received from the victim/s. The offender can be required to seek various kinds of help, make an apology, undertake unpaid community work, attend educational sessions or undergo various kinds of assessment. Often, several of these ingredients will be combined, and the offender has 90 days to complete what is ordered. Sometimes there are subsequent board meetings, but not in all cases (Karp 2002). Since 1999, boards have been available to all courts in Vermont, and they have achieved acceptance among most criminal justice professionals, many of whom were originally sceptical about or hostile to the idea. A small study by the Corrections Department suggested that offender recidivism rates may have improved in these minor cases (Osborne and Plastrik 2000), although this was based on only a small sample and the researchers followed the offenders up for only six months, which is much shorter than the period required for reliable reconviction studies.

At the meetings board members, in introducing themselves, typically try to establish some common ground with the offender and to emphasise that they are volunteers. In the case of offences which might be regarded as victimless, they stress the reasons for community concerns about such behaviour. There is an undoubted imbalance of power in most such meetings, and from the offender's point of view, 'It is generally in their interest to be polite and agree with board members at every turn [because to be] seen as uncooperative…might lead to a more punitive contract' (Karp 2002, p.76).

Commonly, the offender is invited to look at the offence from the point of view of the victim or others who might have suffered as a result of it, often mediated through board members' views and experience in the absence of the victim.

It is noteworthy, though, that in all the examples given in Karp's research, victims do not take part or attend (although one such case is briefly described by Osborne and Plastrik 2000). Sometimes others speak on the victim's behalf, and the overall philosophy of the boards is designed to be reparative, but the higher priority is that 'the moral order has been affirmed' (Karp 2002, p.82). However, victims are routinely informed when offenders complete their obligations (Roche 2003), which is a great improvement on most formal criminal justice disposals. Some offenders are ordered to write essays about why what they did was wrong, and others are warned about what might happen if they re-offend; sometimes, perhaps, in rather a patronising way. The ethos of the panels varies considerably from one part of the state to another, which fits in with a notion of community accountability but is harder to justify in terms of consistency of outcomes. People volunteer to serve on boards

> because they think they can help do a better job. They think the criminal justice system isn't paying much attention to minor crime. They think we ignore the crime that most immediately impacts their lives. They don't want that crime ignored, and they are willing to spend time and effort to deal with it, if we let them. (Osborne and Plastrik 2000, p.2)

Victims might welcome some aspects of the system, but they have not been particularly heavily involved in it so far. They have been directly involved in fewer than 13 per cent of cases where there was a direct victim (Karp 2004; McCold 2004). Examples of community justice such as Vermont's community reparative boards may be partly designed to empower victims, but they do not seem to be as successful in achieving this aim as they might be. As McCold (2004, p.22) scathingly puts it,

> Community justice retains all critical decision-making power in the hands of dispassionate strangers, either justice officials or citizen volunteers who are unrelated to those directly involved. Making decisions and doing things to offenders and for victims, while excluding the families of both, fails to empower anyone but the existing justice apparatus.

Although this statement is made in the context of a polemical defence of the claims of restorative justice to be distinct and superior to community justice, it nevertheless seems valid (but see Bazemore and Schiff 2004 for a contrary view). It is quite possible to hold offenders accountable and encourage them to think about the impact of their behaviour upon victims without victims becoming directly involved, but this is not part of a process of victim empowerment. Nevertheless, research based upon discussion of case studies and a public opinion survey suggests that in Vermont 'victims overwhelmingly favour using reparative boards; indeed, support among them is as strong as it is among nonvictims' (Greene and Doble 2000, p.7).

Significantly, 51 per cent of the people interviewed for the opinion survey (who had been told about what reparative boards were) said that they would attend a board meeting if they were a victim of crime. Before the survey, however, only 13 per cent of them knew about boards, which suggests that the low victim participation rate may be related to a failure to explain and publicise the boards' work adequately (Greene and Doble 2000, p.61). The authors conclude that support will grow as knowledge of the initiative spreads:

> Those who know about the boards have a positive view of them by a margin of 11 to 1 (77 percent to 11 percent). Our findings suggest that as people learn about the reform, they will enthusiastically support the idea (Greene and Doble 2000, p.96)

They also recommend further research on victims' perceptions of the boards, and this would seem overdue. Indeed, it seems strange that public opinion research was not augmented by an attempt to establish the views of victims about the success or otherwise of the initiative from their point of view.

Street committees and people's courts in apartheid-era South Africa

In the 1980s and early 1990s, people in South African townships began to seek alternatives to the white apartheid state's police and courts. A number of models emerged, but these are not discussed here at any length. The purpose of giving this example is simply to contrast these models with the subsequent development of peace committees, which appear to represent a model of community justice in practice (see below).

Rural communities in South Africa had always had their own ways of doing justice based upon African customary law. Community leaders dispensed justice without involving state agencies. To some extent, the alternatives to the methods of the repressive white state apparatus which were devised in townships were in turn based on these rural customs (Roche 2003). While customary law and its successors were undoubtedly preferable to white colonialist justice, which had no legitimacy in black townships, they had considerable shortcomings. Customary law tended to be almost exclusively in the hands of men, and to be administered in paternalistic – indeed, patriarchal – and unaccountable ways. It was open to corruption and bias, it could be arbitrary and it was sometimes extremely harsh (see Chapter Three).

The street committees and people's courts developed in townships represented community justice in the sense that they were administered by local lay people, and they represented a move away from state-run criminal justice.

They had the virtue of informality, and of achieving local support. Because there was no police presence in townships, people's courts had to investigate crimes as well as dealing with the people involved, and this meant that their independence was inevitably compromised (Shearing 2001).[1]

Township justice was often 'owned' and enforced by existing non-governmental organisations such as political parties, street gangs or even sports teams like the notorious Mandela United Football Club (several of whose members were imprisoned in 1991 for offences including kidnapping). It was intensely politicised, as part of the black resistance to apartheid, and this had its dangers. During the political transition period in the early 1990s, problems increased:

> These bodies often were established with the best of intentions, as townships struggled to deal with high levels of crime, and where the formal criminal justice system was both inaccessible and illegitimate. But in an environment of extreme political turmoil and violence, they often departed from their original aspirations and imposed progressively harsher punishments, including severe floggings. (Roche 2003, p.520)

Different informal justice organisations began to compete with one another in turf wars, sometimes engaging in serious crimes such as rape, kidnapping supposed spies, and arson. Ultimately, the Mandela United Football Club and Winnie Mandela were implicated in the deaths of Stompie Seipei and others in 1988, and they were publicly condemned for their excesses in 1989 by anti-apartheid organisations and black churches (Sampson 2000). The MUFC and other townships' informal community justice apparatuses were dismantled or, in some cases, replaced by other, more legitimate, popular structures.

One of these new structures was the peace committees, which used trained and licensed local members as part of an informal justice system to respond to reports of crime and disorder. These committees had been set up in six townships during the first decade of an experimental project, and the programme seems likely to expand considerably. It was initially funded by a grant from the Swedish government. Referrals are mostly received from community members themselves, rather than from formal criminal justice

---

1   The structure of peace committee meetings represents an attempt to remedy this deficit: meetings begin by separating the parties and obtaining each person's account of what happened. These often conflicting accounts are then the basis of the committee discussion, with the parties present, aimed at reaching a consensus about how to repair the harm done (Roche 2003, pp.265–6).

agencies, and committee members (or 'peacemakers') are held to account through the licensing system which monitors their adherence to agreed principles including confidentiality, healing and adherence to the law and the constitution. Victims are invariably involved in the committees' deliberations – and for this reason, peace committees are discussed further in Chapter Three which deals with restorative justice. Building upon and adapting compromised models of community justice, it has proved possible to retain the best aspects of people's courts and street committees while remedying their most glaring faults. The committees have achieved legitimacy within their own communities, as demonstrated by their workloads based upon referrals received from community members, and they have emerged as a possible alternative both to the vigilante approaches which they replaced and to the white-owned official legal system which has little reality for township residents. They provide a means of empowering poor people to take ownership of conflicts, drawing on Christie's ideas about conflict as a potentially positive force (Shearing 2001). Uniquely, they have also developed a system which allows them to help build up communities' capacity to respond to the needs they uncover: part of the fee paid by the government for each case handled goes into a 'peace-building fund' which pays for local environmental improvements, the creation of new community facilities and providing loans to small businesses (Roche 2003).

Circles of support and accountability, Canada and the UK

Circles of support and accountability came into existence partly because of a perceived gap in the statutory provision for supervision and support for sexual offenders released from prison in Canada. Once ex-offenders there who are not eligible for parole are released, these 'warrant expiry' ex-prisoners are not required or entitled to receive any corrections service supervision (Yantzi 2004). However, it became clear in the early 1990s that prisoners who were referred by prison chaplains and psychologists to religious ministers in the community were receiving informal support on an *ad hoc* basis, and in 1994 a pastor in Hamilton, Ontario, who received such a referral decided that he needed assistance in responding positively and effectively to the request to support a released paedophile offender who had previously belonged to his Mennonite congregation. He approached several acquaintances of the ex-offender and other local church-going people to assist on a voluntary basis, including a Neighbourhood Watch volunteer who would represent community concerns about the release of a serious sexual offender to the area (which had become an issue in the local media) (CSC 2001).

The idea originated in work undertaken by another Canadian, Mark Yantzi, who had developed support-accountability groups for sexual offenders in the community within a number of Christian churches. These were based upon the idea that church membership created obligations for such offenders, but that their membership also created obligations for the Church itself. As the then head of the prison chaplaincy, Pierre Allard, put it, the aim was to demonstrate 'the impact of a community of faith on a community of crime' (quoted in Petrunik 2002, p.503). Offenders received access to additional support through their church membership, but this made it possible for the Church to make demands upon them in terms of accountability. Yantzi harnessed the concern of church members in a systematic way, in collaboration with treatment agencies, but the original model was much less intensive than circles of support and accountability, which typically work with more serious offenders (Yantzi 1998). The Mennonite Church recognised the need for more intensive work with serious offenders, and devised a Community Reintegration Project funded on a pilot basis by the corrections service (see Heise et al. 2000; Wilson and Picheca forthcoming).

This kind of initiative was subsequently formalised by Correctional Services Canada (CSC) as part of its community chaplaincy programme, in collaboration with the Mennonite Church. Priority was to be given to those considered to be at the highest risk of re-offending on release and this helped to justify quite intensive intervention in those cases where the ex-offender was willing to sign an agreement (or 'covenant') to participate. The new service was named 'circles of support and accountability', emphasising the twin approach of offering community support and requiring ex-offenders to submit to close supervision in return.

The inclusion of a community representative in the original circle in Hamilton represented an attempt to engage with the concerns of the community, but victims and victims' organisations were sceptical about the initiative and circles of support and accountability have struggled to find ways of reflecting their concerns and views. The Hamilton circle 'recognized victim concerns at least theoretically [but...] this remains an emphasis that requires further development' (Yantzi 2004). This shortcoming had been identified three years earlier in an internal evaluation of the programme (CSC 2001), although some of the local circles had established contacts with victims' groups by that time and this was recommended as a positive development which should be emulated. A few circles had arranged training for their volunteers from victims' advocates, but this was relatively unusual. Thus, although proponents of circles of support and accountability use the rhetoric of restorative justice, circles are only partially restorative because they do not involve victims directly (or indeed, in many cases, indirectly either).

Circles of support and accountability represent a practical attempt to introduce a number of aspects of community justice, despite their frequent failure to engage effectively with victims. They clearly offer a responsible role to volunteers from the communities into which ex-offenders return, as well as providing them with the training and supervision they need to undertake it effectively. These community representatives work alongside professional people in assessing risk, providing support and fellowship, making links to other services and holding ex-offenders accountable. Part of the thinking behind the provision of such a service is the (limited, but developing) research evidence that loneliness, low self-esteem and social isolation are important factors which predict an increased likelihood of re-offending (Bates *et al.* 2004).[2] Re-offending rates are said to be low, although (rather surprisingly) this is based only upon anecdotal evidence from circle members themselves and two more rigorous but small studies by CSC psychologists of circles in Toronto and Ontario. In the Toronto study, recidivism rates were 50 per cent lower than statistically predicted for 30 men (CSC 2001, p.11). In the Ontario study, which looked at 30 circle members and 30 members of a matched control group, reconviction rates were also significantly lowered, and the nature of the convictions was in every case less serious than the offender's previous offences. Reported re-offending of a sexual nature was less than half the rate recorded in respect of the control group (Wilson and Picheca forthcoming).

It is not only less costly to provide such a service using volunteers; it also helps to convince many ex-prisoners of the sincerity of those who are offering to befriend them, and to build the trust which is necessary for such a relationship to be effective (CSC 2001). Most of the volunteers come from faith groups, not only Christian, because the initiative is based in the correctional service's chaplaincy and core members largely become aware of it through personal contact with a prison chaplain. They are carefully screened, and undertake five days' training (Wilson and Picheca forthcoming). Between 1994 and 2000, 42 such circles met in Canada, for periods between 18 months and 6 years. Each consisted of five or more volunteers, the ex-offender

---

2   The Thames Valley research team is also producing unpublished papers taking this work forward. The team can be contacted at the Thames Valley Project in Didcot: see www.thamesvalleyprobation.gov.uk.

and relevant professionals (who do not routinely attend the meetings). Three of the offenders were known to have re-offended – a very low proportion, less than half the statistically predicted number (Petrunik 2002; Wilson and Picheca forthcoming), but the numbers involved in these studies are too small: further research will be required before there can be any certainty about the success of this aspect of the initiative. However, one of the first offenders to be released onto the programme was assessed by the prison psychologist as 100 per cent certain to re-offend within a seven-year period, and he has lived in the community without further convictions for over 10 years (Wilson and Picheca forthcoming).

Circles therefore fulfil some aspects of community justice fully, and others partially. They are characterised by greater informality than statutory supervision, they involve lay people and they are provided in partnership between churches and the state corrections service. They are partly locally controlled, but they do little to reduce professional involvement in resolving difficulties and they are not necessarily less bureaucratic than statutory services (although they are probably experienced by offenders as less impersonal). Given the seriousness of some of the offences involved and the strength of community feeling about the release of sexual offenders, it is perhaps hardly surprising that the central state has taken a cautious approach in relation to circles of support and accountability in Canada.

It is interesting to note that a much more centralised and less liberal penal system exists in England, where a similar programme has been introduced on an experimental basis, initially running from 2002 to 2005. The prevailing punitive climate of criminal justice policy is perhaps one reason why the circles of support and accountability in three pilot areas have taken place discreetly, but evidence is beginning to emerge of their potential for success, both as experiments in community justice and as ways of managing serious sexual offenders in the community.

In the English projects, the 'core member' of a circle of support and accountability (the ex-offender) has usually completed Sex Offender Treatment Programmes while in custody. Referrals to the pilot circles have come predominantly from probation officers and prison chaplains, and most men are visited for an assessment before release. The circle is completed on release by four to six trained volunteers, and it meets weekly at first. That meeting includes a session to plan individual members' contacts with the core member during the coming week, which initially take place at least daily (in person or by phone) and in addition to any requirement to report to statutory agency staff. These contacts often have a practical component: particularly at first, circle members help the ex-prisoner to deal with aspects of resettlement and to develop relationships in the community. Once there is agreement that the ex-offender is becoming 'more secure within society' the frequency of contact is reduced (Naylor 2003, p.2). Circles typically meet formally for a year after the core member's release from prison, sometimes with some informal follow-up. An early task of the weekly meeting is to agree a contract with the core member. Although these are flexible, they usually involve a number of common elements;

- a commitment to openness within the circle
- respect for confidentiality beyond it (within certain conditions about what can be disclosed if public safety is an issue)
- the need to avoid further victimisation and the core member's commitment to this
- the core member's commitment to the agreed release plans
- the ground rules governing the circumstances in which concerns will be expressed to the statutory agencies involved in the supervision of the core member (Drewery 2003).

The contacts from circle members are respectful, non-judgemental and supportive to the core member, while requiring him to give information and participate in discussion about risk factors:

> Regular contact with Circle volunteers enables an offender to feel accepted as a person and to learn to relate appropriately to adults. At the same time the Circle members hold the core members accountable for their actions with the hope that they will develop a lifestyle which does not include offending. (Naylor 2003, p.2)

The reference to appropriate relationships with adults presumably reflects the high representation of sexual offenders against children among those supervised by the circles in the pilot areas (Canadian circles began by prioritising high-risk sexual offenders, but moved on to work with other types of ex-prisoner too).

One volunteer told a journalist reporting on the pilot projects,

> As a volunteer, you can utilise your life skills... It's not as if you have to do anything special – you just have to be a human being. I now don't understand how people can be let out of prison without this kind of support. (Tany Alexander, a Quaker quoted by Fursland 2004)

A core member told a researcher about his circle volunteers: 'They challenge me but they don't judge me', contrasting them with the professionals involved in his supervision for their ability to separate their views about the offence from their attitudes and behaviour towards the offender (Bell 2003, p.24).

Circle members are supported by the relevant professionals and information is exchanged regularly, particularly in cases where the core member is subject to statutory supervision. Volunteers are drawn from a range of sources, but the religious affiliations of the bodies which have established the pilot projects have meant that faith communities have provided a high proportion of circle members. Two of the pilot projects have been set up with the support of local probation areas, and one by the Quakers (building upon the Religious Society of Friends' long history of involvement in criminal justice reforms). Another has been set up in conjunction with a local charity, the Hampton Trust, and the third is managed by the Lucy Faithfull Foundation specifically for former residents of a hostel for released sexual offenders.

The extent to which the core members' participation can be characterised as voluntary depends upon the other conditions of their release: most will be subject to sex offender registration procedures, parole conditions (including the potential for recall to prison if these are breached), and multi-agency public protection panel surveillance in more serious cases. Nevertheless, the voluntary element appears to increase such men's (and occasionally women's) trust in the system and their readiness to discuss their feelings and anxieties, building upon the work they have done whilst imprisoned. Involvement with a circle can mean recall to prison when things go wrong and the risk presented by the core member is assessed as being unacceptably high, but it can also improve such ex-offenders' chances of resettling successfully and avoiding further offending, which appears to have been successfully achieved in a number of the cases handled by the pilot projects (although these have yet to be fully evaluated). As well as meeting the core member regularly, volunteers are trained to negotiate a relapse programme with him or her (based upon the work done whilst in prison) and this forms the main business of the circle meetings. This helps to block any attempts at avoidance – but information about offences is normally shared by the core member voluntarily with other circle members, rather than being supplied to them by statutory agencies in advance. Volunteers' training is based upon what is known about what is likely to trigger a relapse into offending, and they know what signals to look out for as well as how to enhance the core member's motivation to stick to the agreed programme (QPSW 2003). After an initial familiarisation period when only the weekly circle meetings take place, individual contacts between meetings begin.

A high calibre of well-trained and well-supported volunteers is required to make a success of a circle of support and accountability. The dynamic between care and control, support and accountability, has to be continually managed. Sexual offenders can be manipulative, uncommunicative and defensive, and if this is a smokescreen for an intention to reoffend, enforcement action has to follow. This makes considerable emotional and other demands upon volunteers, and they may disagree among themselves on occasion (Clark 2003).

The English variant of circles of support and accountability is perhaps slightly less in accordance with community justice principles than is the Canadian model, but it also caters for more serious offenders. It fails to involve victims, and it involves the volunteers in working closely with the statutory services, but it engages community volunteers in close supervision and support of ex-offenders including people on parole. It is a recent innovation, and only limited evidence is so far available from the evaluative research which was built into the English pilot projects (QPSW 2003). While a relatively high proportion of circles in the first couple of years in England resulted in core members being returned to prison, this might be seen as a success in view of the emphasis on community protection and the seriousness of the offences concerned in the cases of some men released on parole (Wilson, C. 2003). The strengths of the experimental projects lie in the creation of an opportunity for community members to reach out to stigmatised, even demonised, ex-offenders in a structured way which holds them accountable and provides a measure of monitoring and community protection. Circles offer significant support to people who are often lonely and depressed, while challenging their denial and watching out for warning signs (QPSW 2003). If their apparent successes are confirmed by research, and the decision is taken to legislate for national coverage, circles of support and accountability offer a possible way of informing public opinion about the possibility of safe reintegration of sexual ex-offenders after their release from prison (Center for Sex Offender Management 2000).

Circles of support and accountability have been established not only in Canada and the UK, but also in Ireland, The Netherlands and the USA (Wilson and Picheca forthcoming).

A pilot Community Justice Centre in Liverpool, UK

Another community justice project which is at the pilot stage in England is the Community Justice Centre in North Liverpool, based upon a similar experiment in Brooklyn, New York (the Red Hook Community Justice Center, which was set up in 1994 and subsequently caught the attention of the Lord Chief Justice of England and Wales, Lord Woolf (see Woolf 2002), and of British politicians). The Liverpool pilot runs from 2004 to 2006, and it builds upon the US judges' intention to take a more proactive approach to dispensing justice, applying a community approach which 'taps into the problem-solving skills of citizens instead of relying solely on the expertise of professionals. It is localized and flexible rather than centralized and standardized' (Clear and Karp 2000, p.21).

The Red Hook Center is one of a number of 'community court' initiatives in US cities promoted by the Federal Justice Department. They bring together community representatives and judges, supported by the other criminal justice and social welfare agencies, to identify and address crime problems and underlying social problems. Justice is dispensed more swiftly than normal, and there is an opportunity to target particular forms of crime and disorder which affect residents' quality of life. While such projects provide services which might not otherwise be available, they may also criminalise relatively minor anti-social behaviour (Kurki 2000).

The Liverpool project was also influenced to some extent by an earlier model: that of the French Ministry of Justice's Maisons de Justice et du Droit (MJD, literally 'houses of justice and the law'). These were initially set up on an experimental basis in a number of regions in the early 1990s, and then put onto a statutory basis in densely populated areas nationally. They were intended to introduce a new type of courts, which increased public access to – and understanding of – justice. A higher quality of justice was intended to increase social cohesion in urban areas by bringing its administration closer to citizens, improving access to the law, streamlining judicial procedures and attacking the causes of minor anti-social behaviour (Brimacombe 2004). The experiment was undertaken in the context of a long tradition of tackling urban problems through community development, and the MJD programme was intended to encourage innovative approaches (although in practice it appears to have succumbed to pressure from central government to standardise its approach).

The Liverpool experiment has some elements of community justice, but in other ways it is much more wedded to the traditional, authoritarian, state model of criminal justice. At its centre is a 'community justice judge' – perhaps an unusual judge, but a paid judge nonetheless. Lord Woolf has argued that a well-resourced court, working in partnership with other agencies, can reach out to a troubled community and tackle some of the underlying problems which cause crime, as well as dealing with offenders in the more usual ways. The intention is to use a criminal court as an outreach centre, and to involve local organisations and individuals in the delivery of justice. The rationale for giving a judge such a crucial role in the Community Justice Centre seems to be that victims and witnesses have to be protected from intimidation and retribution by offenders, and that the law must be seen to be upheld. This argument was strongly advanced by Lord Woolf and a senior police officer in a round-table discussion about the initiative, but it was opposed by a representative of a community agency:

> In the area that we are talking about, it seems that new initiatives are driven from the top down, and I feel that young people in particular will never come on board, never participate, if they are not at the centre of this. (Frances Lawrence in *New Statesman* 2004, p.vi)

The New York centre combines a problem-solving approach with outreach work aimed at crime prevention. Rather than concentrating on processing individual cases, an attempt is made to ensure that services are available on the spot to defendants whose crimes reflect wider community problems such as drug misuse, unemployment, poor health and poor housing conditions. This approach includes mediation in appropriate cases between complainants and offenders, for example in disputes between landlords and tenants or in some domestic violence cases. Links are made with community agencies, and the centre itself administers or provides a venue for a number of community volunteer projects. The justification for the extra resources required for the New York pilot project is that it 'is about partnership, about communities coming together to solve discrete problems and to promote greater legitimacy in the eyes of the public' (Greg Berman in *New Statesman* 2004, p.vii).

Whether the initiative is effective either in promoting legitimacy or in other ways, remains a largely unanswered question: 'All we know about [...] community courts [...] is based on descriptive case studies or promotional literature that lack critical and evaluative aspects' (Kurki 2000, p.263). Similarly in France, 'Little can be demonstrated about the effectiveness of the community courts either on offending behaviour or on the quality of life in the communities that they serve' (Brimacombe 2004, p.11).

The Liverpool pilot, like its French and American precursors, aims to 'increase community participation and confidence in criminal justice' (Crime

Reduction website 2003), but it was perhaps significant that the press release which announced its establishment emphasised offenders' needs and mentioned victims only once. The Community Justice Centre deals with relatively minor 'quality of life crime' and with anti-social behaviour as well as conventional crime, and it requires an unusual approach from its resident judge. Whereas British judges are generally expected to stay out of the limelight, the Liverpool community justice judge is required to have a high profile and to promote the Community Justice Centre, as well as leading inter-agency initiatives. A specific reference in the judge's job description draws attention to the role of the New York community judge in taking part in

> non-court community activities designed to knit court and community together or to divert people from crime. Evidence from Red Hook has shown this to be a critical aspect of the role of the Judge. (Department of Constitutional Affairs 2004)

Thus, the first judge appointed to the Community Justice Centre started work before the court even opened, attending meetings with local residents, visiting high-crime areas and giving press interviews. He expressed the view that 'The answers will come from within the community... You actually need to be a known face within the community, and that is quite different from a regular judge' (Munro 2004, p.17). This certainly set a very different tone from that of the traditional relationship between English judges and the communities covered by their courts, which is one of extreme circumspection and considerable social distance.

The centre is based on a court, but it also provides offices for workers from a range of other agencies so that the court's orders can be put swiftly into effect. These include the police, prosecution and probation services and the youth offending team. There is a strong emphasis upon witness protection.

Another unusual aspect of the appointment is that the judge is expected to take an active interest in the progress of those sentenced to community penalties and treatment programmes, 'through monitoring their progress personally, establishing real offender accountability and promoting individual responsibility' (Department of Constitutional Affairs 2004). This approach brings the judge closer to criminal justice agencies and individual offenders than would normally be regarded as proper, but it fits in with the high profile required of the judge and the centre's emphasis upon problem-solving approaches. A previous UK initiative which encouraged such an approach by judges and lay magistrates was the Drug Treatment and Testing Order (DTTO). After such an order is made, the sentencing judge or magistrates track the offender's progress at periodic review meetings. The Lord Chief Justice has spoken approvingly about the apparent success of the first two years of DTTOs, which he said had a failure rate of only 29 per cent:

> It is found that the involvement of the judges maintains the motivation of those who are the subject of the orders. They respond to both the deterrent effect and the approbation they receive when they make good progress. The involvement of the judge is not only good for the offenders, it is good for the judges themselves. Their involvement means that they obtain valuable experience as to how to use the orders most effectively. (Woolf 2002, p.11)

He went on to argue that deferred sentences could be used in a similar way, and to refer specifically to the experience of using a similar mechanism in New York. The Liverpool centre's judge made it clear on his appointment that he favoured using community penalties to hold those who committed nuisance offences accountable to the court, and that he intended to become involved in monitoring their compliance with treatment and other conditions in the court orders made (Munro 2004).

The interests of victims are somewhat marginalised in the publicity material as well as in the judge's job description. In the New York model, victims are seen as 'having responsibilities' in that

> their goal is to recover their capacity to fully function in the community. Recovery begins when the victim articulates the losses, intangible as well as tangible, and estimates the resources, financial and otherwise, needed to restore the losses. (Clear and Karp 2000, p.23)

In return, the victim receives community support in the process of recovery. Ideally, in this model, victims become part of a network of mutual obligations. This seems a somewhat naive formulation, and there is a danger that it places new expectations upon victims who may have good reasons for being reluctant to become involved in such a network. The Liverpool experiment may not take the same approach as in New York, and it seems likely that English victims' organisations will defend the principle of victims' right to choose whether or not to be drawn into 'obligations' towards offenders. In reality, the Community Justice Centre seems to offer victims little in the way of new opportunities: they already have the offer of community support in the case of violent, sexual and hate crimes through established voluntary agencies (which are less well-developed in North America). The new model will, however, offer the possibility of mediation and reparation in less serious cases and, as long as this is offered as a real choice, it may assist in resolving disputes and dealing with minor crimes in more creative ways than the current system. It is also likely to increase community expectations of victim support agencies, and this may uncover a need for additional resources for such organisations. Judge David Fletcher said, soon after his appointment to the Liverpool court, that

> traditional court processes often fail to support victims and witnesses, particularly through lengthy trials [...] Victims will be asked for their opinion on an appropriate sentence and given an opportunity to face the offender. He hopes that the speed of the process will encourage greater involvement by victims and witnesses. 'There is a high not-guilty rate in the north Liverpool area, partly because witnesses don't feel comfortable going to court, particularly after time passes', he adds. (Munro 2004, p.16)

The Community Justice Centre represents community justice in that it encourages stronger links between the court and local agencies and volunteers. The ownership of sentencing decisions is retained by a state-appointed, paid judge, but the judge's role is modified to encourage greater outreach to the community and a greater than usual degree of accountability both on the part of offenders and the judge. While some of the lessons learnt in the early days of the Red Hook Community Justice Center have influenced the design of the project, the choice of 'community' in which to experiment in this way appears to have had no particular rationale, and 'the problems of designating and maintaining a community to which a CJC is attached', experienced in the USA and in France, will require attention (Brimacombe 2004, p.11). The role of victims of crime was ill-defined at the outset, and it will be interesting to see how the experiment develops particularly in terms of accommodating the concerns of victims and victims' groups.

The Warwickshire Victim and Witness Information Partnership, UK

A consistent finding of research into the needs and wishes of victims of crime is that they want to be kept better informed than they are under the current system (Mawby and Walklate 1994; Justice 1998; Hoyle et al. 1999; Maguire and Kynch 2000). A number of initiatives have been taken in different jurisdictions in an attempt to remedy this problem, but they frequently suffer from poor communications between the different agencies which have contact with victims and from the low priority given to such contact by agencies such as the police and prosecution services which have other primary objectives (Williams 1999a).

The failure to keep victims informed raises questions about the genuineness of claims that victims' needs are central to criminal justice agencies' missions, and the relevant government ministers in England and Wales acknowledge this (for example in their foreword to, and the section on 'Witnesses' needs' in, the government's strategy to improve services to victims and witnesses, Home Office 2003, and in the *No Witness, No Justice* project, Crown Prosecution Service 2004). They also implicitly accept that services to victims and witnesses will have to improve if more people are to be willing to come forward to report crimes and give evidence: the treatment of victims raises questions about the extent to which the system cares about improving relationships with the community it is ostensibly there to serve. In this context, the source of much of the funding for an experiment in improving information provision is revealing: the Warwickshire Victim and Witness Information Partnership (VIP) received initial funding from the budget of a 'quick wins' committee at the Home Office (the Confidence Task Force) which was charged with increasing public confidence in the criminal justice system. There is clearly some official awareness that providing timely information to victims is an issue relating to the legitimacy of the system in victims' eyes. More recently, the relevant central government agencies have started working together to spread such initiatives through a number of pilot projects under the *No Witness, No Justice* project.

VIP brings together the resources of all the statutory criminal justice agencies and the Victim Support and Witness Support services, as well as a representative of the local multi-agency domestic violence team, in one office. This is staffed outside normal office hours (opening from 8 a.m. to 6 p.m. on weekdays, and on Saturday mornings), and all the agencies share information. The model was developed by a multi-agency Victim and Witness Forum which undertook local research into what was required. The service is proactive in contacting victims and witnesses, which is very different from the experience in most other places, and this was one of the changes made in response to the 2002 National Witness Satisfaction Survey and local focus group research with victims and witnesses. These both found that victims wanted more, and more timely, information about their cases and about the system's expectations of them in terms of court attendance. They wanted to know, for example, how long they were likely to be kept waiting at court, and they wanted to know what ultimately happened to the defendants in their cases. Many people who took part in the local research had taken the initiative in contacting the police and other agencies for information, but they had sometimes been given conflicting and inaccurate information and they complained that there was a lack of continuity, with a variety of people contacting them about different aspects of the case. The national survey showed that victims and witnesses were not told how long they would be required to spend at court, a significant minority (21%) felt intimidated by the process and only a small majority (52%) felt that their contribution was appreciated: overall, many felt that their participation was taken for granted – although the figures have improved slightly since the first witness satisfaction survey in 2000 (Angle, Malam and Carey 2003).

VIP has responded directly to these concerns by ensuring that the outcomes of court cases are communicated swiftly to victims and witnesses (although delays do still occur due to inter-agency communication problems), rapid referrals are made to voluntary victim support agencies where required, take-up of pre-court visits and the offer of support during trials has been increased, witnesses have the option of contacting police officers outside normal hours and take-up of the opportunity to give Victim Personal Statements has increased. The project is being evaluated internally, but no findings have yet been published (Kilgallon 2004).

VIP has some, but by no means all, of the characteristics of a community justice initiative: it involves a partnership between statutory and voluntary criminal justice agencies, and the service has been influenced by consumer research among victims and witnesses. It has, however, been delivered mainly by paid staff, largely due to concerns about confidentiality, and although it is intended to respond to local needs, it is centralised in one town within a large county and it receives few visitors despite providing a drop-in facility. It is an important innovation because it is aimed specifically at victims and witnesses, and it has been able to command resources from central and local government for victim services, partially in response to locally defined needs. It has already proved to be influential in the development of services elsewhere: shortly after it was set up as a local initiative with central government funding, the government established pilot projects under its national Victim and Witness Care programme in five areas. This was followed in 2004 by a requirement that all police and prosecution services co-operate to establish Witness Care Units across the country.

Community justice and 'joined-up government'

Discussion of the merits of community justice has increased the impetus behind the idea of 'joined-up government' in the area of criminal justice. In the UK, a number of factors already encouraged inter-agency work, but the move towards dealing with crime at least to some extent at a more local level and encouraging citizen participation has accelerated the trend towards the creation of a range of new institutions which bring members of different statutory and other agencies together, often alongside ordinary lay people. One intention of the legislators and local practitioners in creating such structures is to improve day-to-day communication between agencies.

In England and Wales, these new institutions have included community safety partnerships and referral order panels. The latter are described in some detail in Chapter Three. They comprise community volunteers alongside a representative of a multi-agency youth offending team, who is normally employed by a statutory agency working with young offenders.

Community safety partnerships (CSPs) are designed to involve people other than the police in the management of crime and disorder problems at a local level. Where they are successful, they promote community activism by existing voluntary agencies as well as more collaborative styles of policing and higher levels of inter-agency co-operation and information sharing. Paradoxically, CSPs in England and Wales were ordained by legislation (the Crime and Disorder Act 1998) and the law requires that they be led by the police and local authorities. They are required to complete regular audits of community safety within their areas and to consult the public and co-ordinate responses to the crime and disorder problems they identify. The legislation does not explicitly require partnership with community organisations and the commercial sector, but this is strongly advocated in the guidance issued on implementation and in regulations. Both these aspects of partnerships are problematic in practice, for a variety of reasons (see Crawford 1998; Hughes, McLaughlin and Muncie 2002).

CSPs do not necessarily involve victim support agencies, but a number of them do so. Carrickfergus CSP in Northern Ireland, Dacorum CSP (Hertfordshire), Glasgow CSP in Scotland, Malden CSP (Essex), Stoke on Trent CSP and West Wiltshire CSP are examples of partnerships which include one or more victim agencies. Apart from Victim Support, some of these CSPs involve Women's Aid groups, domestic violence forums and racial equality councils (all of the examples given are partnerships which have websites where further information can be obtained).

Involvement in such inter-agency networks has undoubted benefits for victim support agencies, but it also costs money and staff and volunteer time. The guidance issued by the government to explain and expand on the legislation encourages those responsible to do what they can to involve voluntary agencies, but organisations such as Women's Aid are not well resourced and it is perhaps hardly surprising that they are represented on fewer CSPs than the much better-off Victim Support. Victim Support representation provides opportunities for networking and exchanging information, including keeping up to date with new developments and ensuring that other agencies are aware of the services they provide to victims.

Community justice and restorative justice

The practice examples of community justice in this chapter have been deliberately chosen to highlight some of the distinctions between community justice and restorative justice (which is discussed in Chapter Three). There has been considerable controversy in the USA about what some see as an attempt to co-opt or take over restorative justice by including it as only one element in the definition of community justice, and there are fears that in the process the 'pure' form of restorative justice will be diluted by calling projects restorative when they only have some of the elements of restorative justice (McCold 2004). Some see Vermont's community reparative boards as restorative, but they commonly lack one aspect of restorative justice, namely the active and equal involvement of the victim alongside the other parties. The same might be said of circles of support and accountability, although there are good reasons for not involving victims directly in the community supervision of serious ex-offenders. Just as 'community justice' is a term covering a very wide range of different levels of community involvement, there is a continuum of 'restorativeness' (see Chapter Three).

There is scope for community involvement in criminal justice without any element of restorative or reparative practice, but there are commonly some overlaps. Any move towards greater community ownership is likely to involve at least including restorative justice initiatives in the repertoire of available sentences or services.

Community justice and victims of crime

Two common themes in this chapter have been the marginalisation of victims' interests and the paucity of evaluations of community justice experiments. These appear to be general problems. The community justice literature abounds in vague references to its benefits for victims, but on close scrutiny it emerges in many cases that victims are only marginally involved or that their inclusion has been an afterthought and was not built into projects' original design. In some community justice projects, victims are hardly mentioned at the design stage, as in the case of community justice centres. In others, claims are made for alleged benefits for victims, but poor project design or delivery results in only a minority of victims having the opportunity to take up their potential for involvement, as in the case of community reparative boards. Other community justice initiatives described in this chapter demonstrate, however, that it is possible to design projects in a way that accepts the centrality of victims' needs: this clearly applies to the VIP in England and to peace committees in several South African townships. The lessons of these community justice initiatives need to be learnt when considering victims as potential beneficiaries of experiments elsewhere. In some cases, it will never be feasible to involve victims directly, as for example in circles of support and accountability – but indirect victim input may well have a lot to offer.

As for evaluation, there are two main problems. In some cases, the research simply has not been done, or it has not been comprehensive or rigorous enough:

> We simply don't know whether any of the various programs that are said to be underpinned by community justice (such as youth aid panels and reparation boards) are successful by any measure that community justice advocates themselves might articulate (even measures short of crime reduction) because so little robust evaluation research has been conducted. (Strang 2004, p.77)

In other cases, there is insufficient respect for the need to learn the lessons of evaluative research. Busy practitioners have other priorities, and policymakers have a tendency to innovate and move on, leaving others to cope with learning and implementing the messages of project evaluations, especially if these are critical of projects' design and the lack of sufficient resources. In practice, political factors may have more influence on decision-making than do positive evaluations and, in a febrile political climate, pilot projects may be 'rolled out' nationally even before the outcome of evaluative research is known (Sanderson 2002; Wilcox 2003). Unless evaluators are independent of the projects being researched, they will often be susceptible to pressures to produce 'good news' and 'quick wins'. Pilot projects can then, at worst, become window-dressing, because the key decisions have already been made. Even if this is not the case, there may well be political pressure to show results from an early stage and to tailor evaluations to extraneous priorities.

With these two substantial provisos – that many community justice initiatives have yet to be fully evaluated, and that victims are often marginalised at the design stage and subsequently – there are nevertheless some potential benefits for victims from community justice. Victims are part of the community to which community justice advocates want to return criminal justice: local projects run by or with local people may well prove beneficial to victims' interests. New projects and new ways of working need not be planned without victim input, and some of the examples given in this chapter (such as peace committees and VIP) show that it is perfectly feasible to include victims and victims' organisations from the outset. Others could improve their practices and adjust their priorities to accommodate and meet victims' needs more effectively, and there is some evidence that this may happen. The evaluators of community reparative boards, for example, have acknowledged that 'an unfortunately small number (13%) of victims participate in board meetings with offenders', although they attribute this to a combination of 'the logistical challenges of implementation and, ultimately, the disinterest [sic] of victims' (Karp 2004, pp.60–1). Elsewhere, the same statistic has been quoted as evidence that boards need to adapt their practices in order to live up to the rhetoric about victim empowerment (McCold 2004).

The community justice model (and in the UK, the official encouragement of joined-up working and effective inter-agency partnership) has also been influential in the design of some victim-centred initiatives such as VIP, but it has also been called in aid of developments such as the pilot Community Justice Centre. The lessons of experiences in other jurisdictions need to be learnt, and it seems from the discussion above that these include the necessity of involving rather than marginalising victims, and the benefits of rigorous evaluative research which takes victims' needs and experiences into account.

Chapter Three

Restorative justice and its implications for victims

The period since the 1980s has seen a worldwide growth of interest in the implementation and possibilities of restorative justice. This chapter suggests that the introduction of restorative approaches to criminal justice has potential benefits for the victims of crime, but that everything depends upon the assumptions underlying such developments, the design of the projects concerned and the extent to which conventional 'gladiatorial' approaches to criminal justice remain in place alongside restorative methods. Despite the rhetoric of inclusiveness employed by the advocates of restorative justice, many restorative justice initiatives have been driven primarily by concern for the welfare of offenders, and it is important to assess their impact upon victims (and instructive to consider how different they might look if they had been designed with victims' welfare and needs as the primary consideration). The extent to which legislation and experimental projects are 'offender-led' or 'victim-led' is proposed as one criterion for evaluating their likely appeal to victims, whose participation is often an important measure of success.

Definitions

'Restorative justice' has been defined in a number of different ways. In essence, it involves trying to restore victims, offenders and the wider community to something like the position they were in before the offence was committed, ideally by involving them all in the decision-making process and, where possible, attempting to reconcile their conflicts of interest through informal discussion. The classic definition was Marshall's (1996, p.37): he argued that restorative justice is 'a process whereby all the parties with a stake in a particular offence come together to resolve collectively how to deal with the aftermath of the offence and its implications for the future', but this definition is not fully inclusive of all the possible approaches to restorative justice. For example, it leaves out shuttle mediation and written apologies (discussed below). It also implies an individualistic model of restoration, which arguably excludes possibilities such as truth and reconciliation commissions with a national remit (Dignan 2005).

Some commentators use the phrase 'restorative justice' more generally to cover any intervention which aims to hold offenders to account by providing opportunities to make amends to victims, either directly or indirectly. However, it is questionable to what extent interventions can be regarded as restorative when, for example, offenders do not know that community work they undertake compulsorily as part of a court sentence is of indirect or symbolic benefit to victims, and the term can be used so loosely as to be almost meaningless (see Curry *et al.* 2004).

Zehr and Mika (2003, pp.41–2) provide a helpful list of what they regard as the essential characteristics and principles of restorative justice. These include the idea that it is important to begin with a recognition that

- 'victims and community have been harmed and are in need of restoration' and, consequently,
- 'victims, offenders and the affected communities are the key stakeholders in justice'
- 'offenders' obligations are to make things right as much as possible' but
- voluntary involvement is preferable: 'coercion and exclusion should be minimised'.

They go on to argue that

- 'the community's obligations are to victims and to offenders and for the general welfare of its members'
- victims' needs should be the starting point of justice
- dialogue should be facilitated, and
- the justice system should be mindful of the outcomes, intended and otherwise, of interventions in response to crime and victimisation.

Their model is deliberately provocative and has a rhetorical element: it is clearly far removed from the reality of most existing justice systems and, indeed, the authors go on to suggest that it is aspirational rather than being descriptive of any current system. Nevertheless, it is useful in providing an ideal type against which to test the claims of particular projects or initiatives to embody restorative principles.

Examples of restorative justice in practice include:

- victim–offender mediation, including mediated apologies and shuttle mediation
- reparation, whether direct to the victim or indirect
- family group conferences
- circle sentencing
- circles of support and accountability
- peace committees.

These are discussed later in this chapter (with the exception of circles of support and accountability, which were discussed in Chapter Two).

Models and motivations of restorative justice reform

A number of commentators in recent decades have pointed to a legitimacy crisis in criminal justice systems in general (Fitzgerald and Sim 1982; Cavadino and Dignan 2002) and in relation to prisons in particular (Woolf and Tumim 1991; Sparks 1994). A legitimacy crisis develops when the confidence of the subjects of criminal justice – victims, offenders and communities – wanes to such an extent that they begin to challenge its fairness and the right of the state to intervene in their lives. If the system is not recognised by those involved in it as fair, just or effective, this creates a political crisis and a search for better alternatives. One response to this crisis has been to consider different methods of resolving conflicts, and moving towards more local and less state-dominated approaches to justice. (Community justice, another kind of attempt to move away from state domination, was discussed in Chapter Two.)

This search for legitimacy is one possible explanation for the enormous growth of interest in restorative justice since the 1980s, and this growth has indeed followed closely upon the identification of the crisis. However, this explanation has its limitations: if restorative justice was envisaged as an alternative to the existing system, it ought to have replaced conventional criminal justice over a period of time rather than blossoming alongside it or even being incorporated as a part of it. In some places restorative approaches have indeed replaced parts of the previous, formal justice system, but elsewhere they have merely supplemented it – and, in any event, the crisis has not noticeably abated. Only in a few countries, for example, have restorative models led to a reduced use of institutional penalties for offenders; although where this has happened, the reduction has been very substantial (as in New Zealand and Austria). These examples are discussed in greater detail later in this chapter.

In some countries, the debate about legitimacy has been fuelled by concern about the justice system's disproportionate impact upon members of minority groups. Here, restorative justice has also appealed to reformers because of a perception that it can help to restore the damaged fabric of disrupted social groups. In Canada, the USA, Australia, South Africa and New Zealand, for example, restorative approaches have been characterised by some of their advocates as facilitating a return to pre-colonial ways of doing justice. Aboriginal cultures have been mined for alternative models of justice which offer possible solutions both to the legitimacy crisis and to the impoverishment, deracination and alienation of many modern native communities. As we shall see later in this chapter, this approach has been criticised as at best sentimentalised and at worst racist, but it has its adherents and its influence has had substantial practical effects in a number of countries.

Another aspect of legitimacy concerns the aspirations, rights and needs of victims. Restorative approaches have been advocated as part of a process of empowering victims and witnesses, bringing them in from the sidelines of the system to somewhere closer to the centre where key decisions are made (Zehr 1990). It has to be said, however, that concerns about the legitimacy of the system in terms of its treatment of offenders have often been more influential. Improving the treatment of victims was a certainly central concern in reforming the youth justice system in New Zealand, but it seems to have been secondary, at least initially, to anxieties about the damage caused by a punitive youth justice system to large numbers of incarcerated young people, including many members of the Maori community (Morris, Maxwell and Robertson 1993, passim; Consedine 1995).

Braithwaite (2002, p.139) points out that the use of victims as 'props by a youth lobby that is concerned only to get a kinder deal for young offenders' has been an issue in the UK, and that 'victims are often enticed into restorative justice before they are ready' in a number of countries (2002, p.140). Both problems can be avoided by introducing appropriate procedural safeguards, but they perhaps reveal an underlying problem of restorative justice being seen as a back door to the introduction of more humane treatment of offenders in a predominantly retributive system. While it is hardly surprising that youth justice workers try to make use of restorative justice in the interests of their young offender clients, victims are bound to be suspicious of restorative justice if they perceive its introduction to be primarily motivated by concerns to treat offenders more fairly and humanely. Indeed, one of the reasons victims give for their reluctance to become personally involved in direct contact with offenders is a concern that the system places the interests of offenders above those of victims. In the early days of family group conferences in New Zealand, there is evidence that a significant minority of victims felt that they were treated disrespectfully and they were less likely to be in full agreement with the conference outcome than any of the other participants (Maxwell and Morris 1993). Their presence had been used to legitimise decisions with which in some cases they clearly disagreed. There were also cases where the alleged benefits of participation were aggressively over-sold, with facilitators urging victims to 'just trust them' (Umbreit and Zehr 2003). Victims are understandably disinclined to suspend judgement in this way, especially if they suspect that the interests of other parties may be given precedence over their own.

Similarly, Hoyle (2002) found that the restorative cautioning experiment in the Thames Valley police area in England[1] had low levels of victim involvement for a number of reasons. Some victims simply wanted to put the matter behind them. Others thought the offence was something that was best left to the police to deal with. Some were concerned about possible further trouble from the offender, and did not want to aggravate matters by taking part in restorative interventions. A substantial number were not consulted about when the meeting would be held, and many meetings were arranged at times which were inconvenient to victims due to their having other commitments such as work. This echoes the reasons given by New Zealand victims in Morris and Maxwell's research: there, too, conferences were often held at inconvenient times for victims. The authors concluded that restorative justice was fundamentally succeeding, but that there were many examples of 'poor practice, especially with respect to practice towards victims' (Maxwell and Morris 2000, p.217). Hoyle goes on to speculate about whether some of her respondents might have welcomed an opportunity to be indirectly involved in

1   A 'caution' is a formal warning from a police officer that a first or minor offence could have led to prosecution and that further misbehaviour will be treated more seriously. Restorative cautioning involves less formal methods, aimed at eliciting a commitment to improved behaviour.

restorative processes (which might include receiving a written apology or exchanging information), but this option was not offered to them. While there will always be victims who want to put offences behind them or who think the police are better equipped to deal with offenders, the other reasons victims gave for not becoming involved in restorative cautioning are all capable of interpretation as arising from an unduly offender-centred approach.

If it were not possible to reassure most victims that the cautioning process was unlikely to result in further trouble from the offender, those approaching victims cannot have been very experienced or confident about the benefits of what they were offering. It is, in fact, very rare for a restorative conference to result in such problems. Indeed, Hoyle found that those victims who received feedback after a conference at which they had not been present reported higher levels of satisfaction with the system and lower levels of anger and fear as a result. The failure to consult victims about when meetings would be held suggests a systemic bias in favour of doing things in ways which were convenient for the professionals involved – the offenders would have little choice about when the meeting was held, either, but in many cases they would be under strong pressure to attend. In practice, the caution could not go ahead without the offender's presence, but the victim's involvement was optional and therefore the efforts to involve him or her took a lower priority.

With these examples in mind, it is perhaps not surprising that Miers' comparative research found that, of the 16 countries whose arrangements he studied, only 1 (Denmark) claimed to be primarily victim orientated and 5 stated that they were primarily offender orientated (France, Norway, Poland, Slovenia and Spain). The remainder described their orientation as mixed. The UK was not included in the study (Miers 2001) but a companion volume looked at seven restorative justice schemes running in England in 1999–2000. This study found that 'schemes' aims and objectives were of two main types: those with a primarily offender-oriented approach, and those which sought to place equal emphasis on the victim and the offender' (Miers et al. 2001, p.17). This reflected the history of some of the schemes, which began as diversion projects for young offenders and later changed into restorative justice projects (but in many cases retained the same management and staff). Changing the culture of organisations is difficult, and it may be some considerable time before the aspiration to place an equal and balanced emphasis upon victims and offenders is achieved in practice in projects with staff originally recruited to work primarily in the interests of offenders. This has been the experience both in the probation service and in youth offending teams in England and Wales as their responsibilities for work with victims have increased (see Williams 2000).

The rise of restorative justice has also been linked to the increasing influence of the political doctrine of communitarianism, particularly in North America and northern Europe since the 1990s. Attempts to put this philosophy into practice have involved trying in various ways to restore civic virtues of reciprocity and neighbourliness and to encourage individual commitment to moral behaviour and a responsible role in the community. Communities are seen as built of individuals and families which have the power to promote positive change. If they have appropriate attitudes, they can 're-moralise' society, however divided and deprived it might be. A communitarian society would be based upon trust, respect, participation, responsibility, solidarity and mutual support, not upon threat, coercion or fear (Walgrave 2002).

This approach has been criticised for sentimentalising a mythical past in which everyone was safe, neighbourly, law-abiding and co-operative (and, it need hardly be added, the heterosexual offspring of a 'complete' family) and for failing to recognise the potentially oppressive nature of informal social control networks such as the family. It is also an implicitly political approach, barely concealing a 'normative and moral project' which buttresses particular attitudes towards social policy such as support for traditional nuclear families and opposition to alternative household models (McLaughlin *et al.* 2003, p.3). In its moral authoritarian guise, it rejects the possibility of analysing social relations in terms of power and structured inequality (Hughes 1996).

When applied to criminal justice settings, communitarian thinking tends to promote community justice approaches, as discussed in Chapter Two. It has also provided an additional impetus to the development of restorative justice (Etzioni 1995): it is closely linked to the notion of 'reintegrative shaming' developed by John Braithwaite (1989). This involves condemning an offence rather than an individual offender, but respectfully shaming the offender and taking timely action which symbolises his or her reintegration into the society of the law-abiding. Like communitarianism, this approach has been criticised for sentimentalising the reality of life in urban societies and exaggerating the potential for community involvement in the rehabilitation of individual offenders.

While Braithwaite (2002, p.154) has acknowledged that reintegrative shaming may operate unequally in practice, he argues that it has to be operated within a framework of legal rights, checks and balances (2002, p.167), and that even the most isolated offender can be assisted if a community with meaning to him or her can be mobilised to effect reintegration.

There does not have to be a pre-existing, cohesive community waiting to welcome the offender back into membership: what he calls 'micro-communities' can be built up to increase offenders' trust, their social bonds, pride in their communities and their personal stake in behaving well, for example through the family group conference process (described later in this chapter). Most offenders will have relationships of trust which can be built upon in both the shaming and the reintegration rituals at a conference. It is a seductive vision. This type of claim is attractive to policymakers seeking 'communitarian solutions for improving social integration and cohesion in an era of radical and unpredictable social transformation' (McLaughlin *et al.* 2003, p.9). It may, however, prove to be unduly ambitious.

While communitarian philosophy has a radical strand which attributes the breakdown of healthy societies to social exclusion and discrimination, it also has an authoritarian tendency (Hughes 1996) which has resulted in criminal justice initiatives such as the parenting order (compulsory parent counselling and parenting classes for those responsible for disruptive children, even when they have committed no offence) and curfew orders (making families responsible for their children's behaviour by ordering them to stay at home between specified hours) in the UK. This needs to be borne in mind when considering the influence of writers such as Etzioni upon the development of restorative justice. Braithwaite himself gives the example of the 12-year-old boy in Australia who agreed – as a result of a discussion at a family group conference – to stand outside a shop wearing a T-shirt on which was printed 'I am a thief'. This might be seen as communitarian, but hardly as reintegrative, particularly when the resultant publicity led to the child and his family being publicly identified. Braithwaite was among those who condemned this interpretation of reintegrative shaming – and facilitator training for those convening family group conferences in the state involved was subsequently adapted in the hope of preventing similar outcomes in future – but it is significant in this case that the proposal came not from the police officer facilitating the conference, but from the boy's mother and the store manager, representing the community, the victim and the offender's support framework (Braithwaite 2002, p.160). New Labour politicians in the UK have applied communitarian thinking to restorative justice in a particular way, introducing an element of coercion which would not fit in well with Zehr and Mika's principles of restorative justice. This is discussed in detail in the next section.

Restorative justice has an international network of enthusiastic advocates in a wide range of (often overlapping) settings; its supporters include members of faith communities, criminal justice practitioners, academic researchers and penal reformers in many countries including some which have not, as yet, begun to implement it. There is also a small, but growing, group of voluntary agencies partly or wholly dedicated to promoting restorative justice, along with a number of commercial providers of training and consultancy. At the European level, practitioners and academics have come together to form the European Forum for Victim–Offender Mediation and Restorative Justice, which has a secretariat in Belgium and runs conferences and a website. A large network supported by the EU is undertaking research into various aspects of restorative justice.[2] These activities are mirrored at the level of individual countries. In the United Kingdom, for example, Mediation UK advocates and publicises restorative justice as part of its wider mission. There is also a practitioners' forum, the Restorative Justice Consortium, which promotes restorative justice in the media and provides training and conferences. Bodies such as the national Youth Justice Board, Crime Concern and Victim Support have appointed restorative justice specialists. Local voluntary agencies such as Remedi in South Yorkshire have been set up to run specific projects. In this way, is becoming institutionalised.

As McLaughlin *et al.* (2003, p.9) point out, this international network has been strengthened by its ability to bring together activists, academics, policymakers and practitioners in a way that 'popularizes the "good news" about restorative justice through conferences, seminars, publications, newsletters, websites and so on'. Although the network contains many who are sceptical about some of the claims made for restorative justice, their involvement contributes to the impression that there is a substantial social movement behind restorative justice. Much of the literature emerging from this activity, however, has an almost evangelical enthusiasm about it, and there is a tendency to characterise restorative justice as the polar opposite of conventional, retributive justice – which it is not (see for example Casey 1999; Pollard 2000). It is important, therefore, to maintain a critical stance in relation to the claims made for restorative justice.

---

2   The European Science Foundation supports COST Action A21 (a co-operation
      on science and technology network on research, theory and evaluation in relation
      to restorative justice): see Goodey 2005; www.kuleuven.ac.be/research/
      researchdatabase/cooperation/C395362.htm.

Problems of design and implementation

Involuntary involvement

It is widely agreed that restorative approaches to criminal justice work best if participation is voluntary for all the parties involved (Graef 2000; Morris and Gelsthorpe 2000; United Nations 2000, para. 7; Wright 2000; Umbreit 2001; Williams 2001; Youth Justice Board for England and Wales 2001). In particular, the involvement of reluctant or disgruntled offenders in direct contact with victims is likely to reveal their insincerity or resentment, and contact with such offenders is unlikely to assist victim restoration. However, Zehr and Mika (2003, p.41) argue that, while it is best if 'coercion and exclusion are minimised [nevertheless...] offenders may be required to accept their obligations if they do not do so voluntarily'. Braithwaite acknowledges that supposedly voluntary participation by offenders is often, in fact, a case of Hobson's choice: the alternatives are worse than taking part in restorative processes, no matter how profound the offender's misgivings might be. He argues for a compromise position:

> my hypothesis is that restorative justice works best with a specter of punishment in the background, threatening in the background but never threatened in the foreground. Where punishment is thrust into the foreground even by implied threats, other-regarding deliberation is made difficult because the offender is invited to deliberate in a self-regarding way – out of concern to protect the self from punishment. This is not the way to engender empathy with the victim, internalization of the values of the law and the values of restorative justice, the sequences of remorse, apology and forgiveness that...can transform lives... (Braithwaite 2002, pp.35–6)

Braithwaite's position is both a pragmatic and a principled one: the implied threat of punishment as a default position helps to improve participation rates without sabotaging the objectives of eliciting empathy for victims and encouraging thinking about pro-social alternatives to offending, and offenders' right to refuse to participate is safeguarded. Perhaps, as Eliaerts and Dumortier (2001, p.213) argue, the idea of voluntary participation is illusory and deceptive, given that offenders in many jurisdictions lose their legal rights to a large extent once they become involved in restorative justice processes. What is clear is that only offenders who accept responsibility for their behaviour (to a greater or lesser extent) should be let loose upon their victims in direct mediation (see Pelikan 1999 on how this is managed in Austria; Umbreit 2001 on the US experience; Tickell and Akester 2004 on Australia).

To put victims in the position of taking part in mediated contact with unrepentant offenders or offenders who deny their guilt is potentially a form of revictimisation, and this is wholly avoidable. The relationship between repentance, empathy towards victims and offenders' future behaviour is a complex one about which relatively little is known: see Chapter Six.

Unfortunately, those who framed New Labour criminal justice legislation in England and Wales in the late 1990s paid little regard to the lessons that have been learnt in other countries about the impracticability of coerced involvement in restorative interventions by offenders. The 1998 Crime and Disorder Act, which combined the introduction of a number of new community penalties aimed at diverting young offenders from prison with sentencing powers that increased the number of young people being imprisoned, also included provisions to compel young offenders to undertake direct and indirect reparation to their victims. Initially, this was a popular sentence with magistrates, and in some areas Reparation Orders were given despite evidence that the young offender involved was reluctant to engage in reparation, or in the absence of information about the victims' views on the matter (Dignan 2001). Courts have considerable powers under this legislation and this discretion has sometimes been used in ways which could have led to coercion of both offenders and victims. This was a direct result of the way in which the Crime and Disorder Act was framed: it enshrined an 'authoritarian' model of restorative justice (Wright 2000, p.21) and

> the offender is not given the chance to *offer* reparation, but is ordered to make it [...the law] considers first the action to be taken in regard to the offender [...] and only then does it say that the attitude of the victim(s) should be ascertained. (Wright 2000, pp.21 and 27; emphasis in the original)

However, youth justice practitioners have generally found ways to avoid such outcomes, instead returning the offender to court for re-sentencing, negotiating with victims in advance or arranging indirect reparation. The national regulatory body, the Youth Justice Board for England and Wales, also issued guidance which made it clear that practitioners should avoid creating situations in which either reluctant offenders or unwilling victims become involved in restorative interventions. Despite the intentions of the legislators, it has been made clear that the principle of voluntary involvement should be upheld: 'the process has to be voluntary for all those involved' (Youth Justice Board for England and Wales 2001, p.1). The law remains in force but it is now relatively little used.

This is because the Reparation Order was largely superseded by the introduction, under the 1999 Youth Justice and Criminal Evidence Act, of the Referral Order. This involves routinely sending almost all young people who appear in court for the first time before a Youth Offender Panel, comprising community representatives and a youth justice worker and charged with reaching agreement on a contract which 'should always include reparation to the victim or wider community and a programme of activity designed primarily to prevent further offending' (Crawford and Newburn 2003, p.62). While the underlying principles of this sentence are restorative, the blanket assumption that reparation of some kind will always be appropriate effectively sidelines any notion of consent by the offender. It is also made clear within the legislation that young offenders have no right to legal representation as part of the panel process. Thus, the New Labour government's commitment to 'responsibilisation' of young offenders has been entrenched in the criminal justice system, albeit ostensibly in the name of victim empowerment. This is an example of restorative justice being used rhetorically to justify a strategy which derives from a number of other philosophical approaches, including an authoritarian version of communitarian philosophy, simultaneously with its acknowledged restorative influences. As Crawford and Newburn (2003, p.239) conclude, 'Coercion provided the capacity to move certain restorative values to the very heart of the youth justice system, and the loss of voluntariness was the price paid' in the process of introducing Referral Orders in England and Wales. The reduction in the numbers of Reparation Orders being made since Referral Orders came into force also suggests that few young offenders are being given a 'second chance' if they do not engage successfully with Referral Orders.

In many ways, nonetheless, the Referral Order has been successful and it has introduced restorative justice ideas and principles to a much wider audience, including volunteer panel members (who are unfortunately, not very representative of the communities they serve in terms of race, gender and class composition – see Crawford and Newburn 2003 for statistics on race and gender). It has removed power from courts and criminal justice professionals to some extent and created new, relatively informal ways for community members to take responsibility for providing restorative responses to youth offending. It has also created opportunities for victim involvement in youth justice, although levels of take-up have been low, perhaps partly because of the philosophical conflicts discussed earlier.

Low levels of victim involvement

The legitimacy of restorative justice as an alternative to conventional criminal justice depends to some extent upon the willingness of victims to take part. In fact, low levels of victim participation are a recurrent theme of the evaluative literature on restorative justice – although this does not apply everywhere. It appears that where restorative approaches are institutionalised rather than experimental, victims are more inclined to take part. There may also be a relationship between the extent to which victims see restorative justice projects as offender-led and their willingness to take part. Another explanation (which is more relevant in some places than in others) is that some restorative justice projects deal predominantly with very minor offences, and there is little incentive for victims to take part in negotiations with young offenders about minor offences of theft or criminal damage (McIvor 2004).

What needs to be recognised – and perhaps this is not always the case – is that victims take a significant risk by agreeing to take part in restorative justice. The risk may have become exaggerated in their own minds, and victims' perception of the threat presented by offenders often reduces as a result of a direct encounter with them. Nevertheless, most victims are likely to be apprehensive about further involvement with offenders, and a failure to take account of this is likely to lead to high refusal rates when victims are invited to take part in restorative processes. It is important not only how participation is presented to victims (it should not be over-sold, but neither should risks be dismissed), but also that safeguards are in place. Despite the controversy about police involvement in restorative programmes, it seems that many victims feel safer taking part in them when they are arranged on police premises, for example (Braithwaite 2002). A discussion paper produced by the Ministry of Justice in New Zealand (1995) suggested that victims commonly gave emotional reasons for not wanting to become involved in restorative interventions: either they did not feel emotionally involved (as in the case of much minor property crime) or they felt emotionally vulnerable (as in many cases where victim and offender are known to each other or where violence was involved).

Some project evaluations have attempted to establish why victim participation rates were lower than anticipated. One rather obvious reason (mentioned earlier in this chapter) is that programmes do not always prioritise victim involvement. If meetings are arranged without consulting victims, for example during the working day, many will simply be unable to attend. This seems to have been a factor in the early days of family group conferences in New Zealand, where only 6 per cent of victims actively chose not to meet the offender, but victims attended in only 51 per cent of cases. Most of those not taking part said they had not been invited, they were given insufficient notice or the conference was held at an inconvenient time (Maxwell and Morris 1993).

Preparation is clearly important, and this is partly an issue of resources. Facilitators who spend time with the parties prior to convening a meeting often find that this is a very intensive process: Jackson (1998) for example reports that family group conference co-ordinators spent an average of 23 hours preparing the participants for the meeting. In the restorative justice pilot projects funded by the Youth Justice Board from 2000 to 2001, the projects in which the police initiated contact with victims had lower levels of victim participation than those where contact was made by other members of youth offending teams. Project evaluators attributed this to the fact that the police were unlikely to have much time to spend on the task and often had not been trained to undertake victim contact work (Wilcox and Hoyle 2002, p.4). Their (often unspoken) attitudes towards the likely benefits of involvement in conferences were probably negative in many cases, and this no doubt coloured the way in which they approached victims about the idea. Where victim attendance rates are high, as in the Reintegrative Shaming Experiments (RISE) project in Australia, this is attributed to positive attitudes by staff, reassurance and adequate preparation, as well as a willingness to accommodate victims' needs in terms of when meetings are held (Strang 2002).

Victim participation levels have been particularly low in the case of Referral Orders, as mentioned in the previous section: only 13 per cent of cases initially involved a victim attending a panel meeting. This has been attributed to a lack of time to prepare the victims for panel meetings and a lack of appropriate training and commitment to victim involvement among those making contact with victims. Panels in some cases also avoided strenuous efforts to involve victims because of the resource implications, although there are signs that victim involvement is now being given greater emphasis and priority. Victims were often given insufficient information on which to decide whether to attend, and those who did take part did not always receive appropriate preparation or support (Akester 2002; Crawford and Newburn 2003). Putting all these factors together, it does appear that this is a case of offender-led policymaking: insufficient thought and resources were put into meeting the needs of the victims. Where this was done, participation rates were higher: Tickell and Akester (2004) give the example of Camden and Enfield youth offending teams in London, where specialist staff and volunteer mediators offer intensive support to victims and participation rates are more than four times the average.

'Traditional' justice

In a desire to introduce fairer systems of criminal justice with more relevance to all sectors of the community, a number of countries have experimented with alternative models drawn – however indirectly – from pre-colonial justice systems. In some countries, these persisted despite the imposition of white colonial systems; elsewhere, they were revived or drawn upon despite having previously been forcibly abolished. Many have welcomed these developments because they appear to respect indigenous cultures and show a willingness to consider radical alternatives to failing methods of doing justice. However, these kinds of adaptations of traditional justice have also been heavily criticised.

Policy transfer from one culture to another is bound to be difficult, and there is plenty of evidence that it often has unexpected consequences (Dolowitz, Greenwold and Marsh 1999; Findlay 2000b). Even within a single country, attempts to transplant a particular approach or project from one context to another can be problematic. Indeed, some of the most successful examples of modifying traditional justice for modern circumstances have their problems: for example, in Australia, restorative justice practices, based to some extent upon previous indigenous approaches, have proved extremely disadvantageous for Aboriginal people. Far from replacing the modern punitive system, restorative justice has grown up alongside it, and the bifurcation of the system between punitive and restorative approaches has meant more Aboriginal offenders being imprisoned (Braithwaite 2002; Cunneen 2003). Similarly, in New Zealand, family group conferences

> emerged in the 1980s, in the context of Maori political challenges to white New Zealanders and to their welfare and criminal justice systems... But the devising of a (white, bureaucratic) justice practice that is *flexible and accommodating* towards cultural differences does not mean that conferencing *is* an indigenous justice practice. (Daly 2002, p.201, emphasis in original)

As Daly points out – along with other commentators such as Blagg (1997, 1998), Cain (2000) and Maxwell and Morris (1993) – restorative justice advocates have sometimes used historical and anthropological evidence selectively in support of their arguement that restorative practices are preferable to retributive justice. In doing so, they have over-simplified both history and the contemporary situation. This might not matter if the sentimentalised version of history provided by writers such as Consedine (1995) and to a lesser extent Wright (1996) were not so Eurocentric and if it had not been so influential on actual practice, as has the false polarisation of restorative and retributive justice. In fact, as Cunneen has pointed out, the two types of approach are capable of co-existing within the same criminal justice system, while the myth of venerable, ancient origins serves to legitimise modern practices. This kind of 'orientalist appropriation of indigenous justice practices' (Daly 2002, p.201) is doubly offensive in the light of its often detrimental impact upon Aboriginal and poor communities (Skelton 2002).

Traditional justice appears, from historical accounts and from descriptions of how it works in practice in some countries, to have some problematic aspects. It is often paternalistic and it gives considerable power and legitimacy to elders or leaders who may not be representative of their communities. In extreme cases, this has led to crime and abuses being covered up rather than opened out for communal debate, because the state has conferred extraordinary power upon 'community leaders' in the name of devolved justice (see Braithwaite 2002, p.158 for examples). Traditional justice can also be extraordinarily vengeful, including penalties such as banishment or corporal punishment (Consedine 1995; Tauri and Morris 1997; Findlay 2000a; Roche 2003), and at times it has been necessary for more humane maximum penalties to be imposed by the state. Revenge does not sit well with restorative justice, as it fails to restore relationships between victims and offenders, although punishment is regarded as compatible with restorative justice by many commentators (Daly 2000; Braithwaite 2002; Crawford and Newburn 2003; for contrary arguments see Wright 1991).

In England and Wales, a bifurcation of the type described in Australia by Cunneen has occurred in relation to young offenders and their victims, but it has been accompanied by a general increase in state intervention in the lives of young offenders and potential offenders. Many of these changes have been heralded as 'restorative'. Almost all first-time young offenders are now referred by the Youth Court to Youth Offender Panels, discussed above. There is a presumption in favour of reparation as part of the contracts agreed between young offenders, panels and (where they are present) victims. Consent is not necessarily sought from the parties; this neglects a basic principle of restorative justice and may lead to a range of difficulties for victims. In the case of Reparation Orders, which are widely believed to have been based upon restorative practices in New Zealand, consent on the part of offenders is legally not an issue at all. This demonstrates the danger that the popularly attractive notion of restorative justice can be deliberately co-opted – and in the process, perhaps discredited – as part of a particular political agenda. As Morris (2002a, p.611) rather polemically argues,

> there are too many schemes which claim to be examples of restorative justice but which fail to meet its key values. The label 'restorative justice' must be treasured; otherwise poor practices will continue to provide ammunition for critics to undermine it.

The role of the police

The role of the police in a number of restorative justice initiatives illustrates the problem identified by Morris. In some jurisdictions, the view has been taken that the police have a part to play in restorative justice, but that it should not normally be a central role because of the need for a neutral, impartial facilitator for direct meetings between victims and offenders. Elsewhere, however, the initiative has been seized by the police, who have to a large extent taken charge of the development of particular projects. Given that the original aim of modern restorative justice was to reduce the role of the state and increase communities' own problem-solving abilities (Christie 1977), this seems somewhat paradoxical, if not unacceptable on principle. Ashworth, for example, argues that

> It is not appropriate for the police to take on what is a quasi-judicial role, when they are so heavily involved in investigations. More strongly, it is inappropriate for the police to be involved in any 'shaming' of offenders. (2002, p.591)

Other objections to police officers taking the role of facilitator in restorative meetings include the potentially intimidating nature of their status as authority figures (particularly where younger people are involved) and the potential for misuse of information gained during such meetings. An especially stark example of the latter problem was revealed in the early days of the police-led 'restorative cautioning' initiative in the Thames Valley area in England, when the project evaluators discovered that police officers had delivered 'restorative' cautions in ways which were calculated to humiliate young offenders and had even, in some instances, attempted to recruit them as informants during cautioning meetings (Young and Goold 1999; Young 2001). This is a very clear illustration of the need for an independent element in the delivery of restorative programmes, which is a legal requirement, in the case of sentences, under the European Convention on Human Rights (Ashworth 2002).

Cautions, of course, are not sentences; but the same safeguards should arguably be applied to the pre-sentence stage. At times, the police also find it difficult to act restoratively, for example by dominating discussions to the exclusion of other parties, and this tends to reduce participants' feelings of having been treated fairly (Young and Goold 1999).

From victims' point of view, such police practices are not perhaps particularly important. However, other problems with the Thames Valley model directly affect their interests. First and foremost, the dominance of the process by the police seems contrary to the restorative justice principle of empowering the parties directly concerned. The researchers evaluating the scheme noted that facilitators sometimes attempted to encourage participants to stick to the 'script' which they used to standardise their own contribution: if people were 'off-message' they were sometimes prompted to conform. This discouraged spontaneous expressions of independent views and must have made it difficult for the parties to express themselves fully. In the absence of victims, the harm done by minor offences was sometimes 'talked up'. As Young and Goold note, this is part of a process described in policing research as 'case construction', whereby certain 'facts' are emphasised and others filtered out as part of the process of building a legal case. Inevitably, such a process will misrepresent victims' views and wishes in some cases. Indeed, the evaluators expressed a fear that the process might become discredited in the eyes of participants because of these problems. It is fair to add, however, that the Thames Valley Police responded positively to these findings and modified both the 'script' and the guidance and training received by the officers involved.

Another largely police-led project involving young offenders and their victims which has been independently researched was a restorative conferencing scheme in Wagga Wagga, Australia, from 1991 to 1994 (Moore and Forsyth 1995; Umbreit and Zehr 2003). The cases selected for referral to the project were decided at the discretion of the police, conferences were convened and chaired by uniformed police officers, and the investigating officer was normally also present and in uniform. A modified programme was established in 1997, run by a Youth Justice Conferencing Directorate which is part of the state's Department of Juvenile Justice (Miers 2001). The original programme was criticised for its insensitive treatment of victims on a number of counts, not all of which apply to the post-1997 arrangements. However, the Wagga Wagga model was influential both in Australia and in the USA, where projects have been based upon it, so these criticisms remain important.

- Participants were not always carefully prepared for their involvement in conferences (partly because some of those running the project felt that spontaneity was a valuable element of the meetings).

- Offenders were brought into the meeting with their supporters first, and they were often invited to tell their story first.

- Victims were strongly encouraged to participate, and in some cases the potential benefits of involvement were 'over-sold' to them (Umbreit and Zehr 2003, p.73).

- The process followed a prescriptive 'script' which discouraged spontaneity in a way which was insensitive to individual differences and to cultural variety.

- Conference facilitators were trained in this approach, but not necessarily in mediation or conflict resolution skills (Umbreit and Zehr 2003, p.74).

It is clearly in victims' interests to be fully and honestly briefed about what may happen during a family group conference; to be given choices about how the meeting is run; to be allowed to say what they want when they want, within reason, and to be supported by appropriately trained staff. It may be that all these conditions could be met in a police-led family group conferencing project, but this was not apparently the case in Wagga Wagga. Although both victims and offenders express high levels of satisfaction with the conferencing process, the levels of satisfaction among offenders and their supporters were much higher than those of victims (Miers 2001). One argument for police-led restorative justice is that this will accelerate changes in police occupational culture in favour of restorative justice (Braithwaite 2002), but this is an argument which has more to do with advocacy for restorative justice than with victims' needs. (For a detailed description of the various conference processes and their difficulties and benefits, see Masters 2002a. Overall, he is positive about the victim experience of conferencing: more positive findings about projects elsewhere are discussed in the following section.)

In Ireland, where the police (*gardai*) facilitate restorative conferences and supervise young offenders under the Children Act 2001, doubts were expressed in parliament about their independence and neutrality in this role, and these were echoed by the Children's Legal Centre and the probation officers' union (O'Dea 2000). The argument centred on the need to protect the legal rights of young people and the desirability of conferences being facilitated by people seen as independent because of the need to hold the ring between state agencies and families' ability to make decisions for themselves.

However, the police officers administering restorative cautions are specialist, specifically trained, plain-clothes officers who have volunteered to undertake this role. Victims (and, in some cases, offenders) are reported to find police involvement reassuring, and in practice they have praised the even-handedness and confidentiality with which the service operates (O'Dwyer 2001, 2004).

Successful innovations

Family group conferences

Despite all the reservations expressed in the previous section, the introduction of family group conferences in the youth justice system in New Zealand has been a success, not only for young offenders but for victims as well. It has undoubtedly led to a reduced use of institutional penalties for offenders, which may well prove to be beneficial for victims in the long term because this will reduce rates of re-offending and thus lessen the risk of future victimisation. After an initial period during which the findings of research were ambivalent about its effectiveness, the system has settled down and it is now evaluated consistently highly by victims and offenders alike. Where young offenders are concerned, family group conferences have largely replaced the formal criminal justice system except in the most serious cases (where defendants will usually attend a conference before going to court), and a number of local experiments have begun aimed at introducing restorative responses to offending by adults (Miers 2001).

Under the New Zealand model, family group conferences are fairly informal meetings convened by neutral facilitators. They usually involve family members and other people supporting the young offender, victims and their supporters, and a police representative as well as the facilitator. They aim to reach a consensus about how best to meet the victim's interests and create opportunities for the young person to make amends. The offender and his or her supporters generally withdraw from the meeting at some stage in order to devise a proposed strategy for making amends. The most common outcomes are apologies and indirect reparation to the community, but many conferences also reach agreement about direct reparation, attendance by the offenders at programmes or compensation. About 5000 conferences are held each year. Those which conclude with apologies have been found to be particularly likely to reduce re-offending. The victim benefits by knowing more about the processing of his or her case, receiving reparation and experiencing 'closure' and reduced anger and fears; most victims reported feeling better as a result of their involvement (as did about half of the offenders). Where victims have not been involved, the reason for this has typically been a failure to meet their needs in terms of involving them in the setting of dates and venues for meetings, and the evaluators have concluded that the issue is more one of poor practice (regrettably, particularly prevalent where programmes involving victims are concerned) than one of the processes or principles of the model (Morris and Maxwell 2000).

A range of rather different models is used in Australia. The most rigorously evaluated of these is in Canberra, where police-run conferences based upon the Wagga Wagga model achieve high rates of satisfaction among both victims and offenders (Strang 2002). The Reintegrative Shaming Experiments (RISE) project was set up to test Braithwaite's theory (discussed earlier in this chapter). The project is unusual in a number of respects. It employs police-led family group conferences for a wide range of offences, including drunken driving and assaults committed by adults as well as violent and property offences by young people. It was evaluated over a five-year period (1995–2000) and cases were randomly assigned to the conferencing programme, allowing genuinely valid comparisons to be made of outcomes from court cases and conferences (although the design was strictly speaking only quasi-experimental since victims were not the primary unit of analysis; see Strang 2002). The research showed high levels of victim satisfaction with the conferencing process, although the victims of more serious offences were both more likely to take part in conferences and more likely to be dissatisfied afterwards. Almost all the victims surveyed wanted and welcomed apologies from the offenders. Those who participated in conferences reported reduced levels of anger and fear of revictimisation, and more of them felt that they had been treated fairly. Most said that they would take part in such a process again, and that they would recommend others in the same position to do so. Victims of violent crime, who perhaps have the most to lose from taking part in a conference where they are confronted with the offender, also have the most to gain in the sense of achieving 'closure' and an accommodation with the offender that assuages their fears. Victims rarely attend court, whereas large numbers of victims attended conferences and were thus much more likely to know the outcomes of cases and ten times as likely to receive some form of compensation or recompense from offenders. In the part of Australia concerned, the law requires that victims be kept informed of the outcomes of cases, but the research found that this occurred in only 14 per cent of the cases which went to court as compared with 79 per cent of conferences (Strang 2002).

Offenders taking part in conferencing were found to have increased respect for the police and the law, and overall their rates of re-offending have reduced[3] (although this varies dramatically by offence type, with violent offenders significantly less likely to be caught offending again during the follow-up period but higher rates of re-offending for drink-driving adults; see Sherman, Strang and Woods 2000).

The RISE experiment is now being replicated at various stages of the criminal justice process in England, in a project funded by central government and run by the Justice Research Consortium with help from the RISE research team. It is being evaluated by Home Office researchers and the findings, particularly if positive, are likely to be highly influential (see www.sas.upenn.edu/jerrylee/jrc/about.html).

Victim–offender mediation

In Austria, both adult and young offenders can be diverted from court for victim–offender mediation at the discretion of the prosecutor. Trained, professional mediators assess cases and arrange face-to-face mediation in most cases where both parties agree to take part, encouraging them to reach an agreement which usually includes some form of compensation (often substantial) or restitution. Tens of thousands of cases have been dealt with in this way each year since the 1980s including, more recently, domestic violence offences, although this has been controversial. Rates of victim participation and satisfaction are high, particularly where young offenders are concerned, and research in the early 1990s showed that re-offending rates have decreased in cases where mediation is used (Pelikan 1999, 2000; Miers 2001). Mediation has become a routine response to juvenile offending, accounting for 20 per cent of cases of violence and property offences on which action is taken, and the Austrian model has influenced developments elsewhere in Europe: for example, the EU has decided that member states should seek to promote mediation in appropriate criminal cases and ensure that mediation agreements are taken into account by sentencers (EU Council Framework Decision on the standing of victims in criminal proceedings, 15 March 2001; see Miers 2001, p.84; Goodey 2005). Similar national systems are already in place in Slovenia, Belgium, France, Norway and Poland.

---

3   For reduced re-offending rates in relation to restorative justice generally, see Latimer, Dowden and Muise (2001); Nugent, Williams and Umbreit (2003); McIvor (2004).

Experimental restorative justice projects are also appearing in a number of European countries in response to encouragement from the EU and European practitioner organisations. The Czech Probation and Mediation Board, for example, has set up pilot projects diverting offenders from court for mediation; in Denmark, the Crime Prevention Council has set up police-led pre-court mediation projects in three areas (Miers 2001). Such projects can be expected to proliferate, both because aspirant EU members see restorative justice as a way of demonstrating their commitment to modernise their criminal justice systems, and because of the success of the international network of restorative justice advocates discussed earlier in this chapter.

Shuttle mediation is an alternative to direct meetings where one or other party does not want this. Victims can obtain information and a measure of reassurance through such a process. This indirect form of victim–offender mediation does not feature in the restorative justice literature to any great extent and many practitioners appear to view it as a second-best alternative, although victims may prefer it for a number of reasons (Hoyle 2002). It is likely to seem less risky than a face-to-face meeting, especially in cases of interpersonal violence. Where it involves a conference in the victim's absence, it is clearly important that the facilitator keep the victim informed of the process and outcomes. Where non-attending victims were given such information, in the case of 'restorative cautions' in the Thames Valley, they were more likely than other victims to be satisfied with the process and less likely to remain fearful of or angry with the offender. However, victims were kept informed in this way only in a minority of cases (Hoyle 2002). Hoyle concludes that it would clearly be better if practitioners conceptualised victim involvement as a continuum rather than a simple black-and-white choice: for many victims, partial involvement can be satisfactory and helpful. In some cases, victims' needs may be met in the process of preparing for a mediation session which they decide not to attend: there are indications that this is one reason for low levels of direct victim involvement in some restorative projects in England (Masters 2002b). In Austria, indirect mediation is a routine response to property offences 'where victims are less likely to need to resolve their feelings' (Tickell and Akester 2004, p.64), but there is still something to be gained from encouraging offenders to think about consequences and victims.

Apologies

The evidence suggests that written apologies from offenders are valued by victims as long as they are produced by offenders themselves. The tone of such letters is important: if they seem sincere, victims may find them very affecting and reassuring – but they do not appreciate letters which have been corrected or tidied up by people working with the offender. They also resent such letters being used for other purposes than those for which they were prepared – such as mitigation in court (Miers *et al.* 2001). Offenders may favour writing a letter because they feel it is a sufficient response, because they cannot face a direct meeting or because the victim refuses such contact. Particularly in the case of younger offenders, an element of oversight may be necessary to ensure that unhelpful letters are not sent, and the preparation of a letter of apology can be part of the supervision process, allowing discussion of why particular phrases might not be constructive from the victim's point of view. Letters are not normally sent directly to victims, who may not want their addresses disclosed to the offender. In some cases, they are not sent at all, but used to try and encourage the offender to reflect on the consequences of their actions.

Peace committees

As noted in Chapter Two, it was necessary to dismantle some of the mechanisms for informal community justice which had developed in South African townships towards the end of the apartheid era, because they had begun to get out of control. They were replaced in some areas by new arrangements which built upon what had been learnt from the previous system and still offered an alternative to state criminal justice. Based upon the ideas of the restorative justice movement, and assisted by some of its proponents, the Community Peace Foundation (since re-named the Community Peacemaking Programme) developed the idea of peace committees (Braithwaite 2000; Shearing 2001; Roche 2003).

Peace committees involve township residents in adjudicating between parties to disputes, including criminal offences. Committee members are trained and held accountable, both by being required to subscribe to a code of practice and by an accreditation system involving a four-monthly renewable licence which can be withdrawn. There is a strong emphasis upon respect for the human rights of everyone involved. Members are paid, but only indirectly: they receive preferential treatment when it comes to the allocation of grants and loans from the fund which makes payments to peace committees in recognition of their work, in order to promote economic regeneration within townships. Most meetings are convened at victims' request and victims invariably take part in them. They are usually held within a few days of the alleged offence or misconduct. Where there is no police presence (which remains the case in many townships) committees conduct informal investigations of offences and of the causes of disputes, although in theory the importance of separating investigation from problem-solving is recognised (Shearing 2001). Proceedings are informal, and the system is designed to address underlying issues (such as poverty or the lack of play facilities: see below) as well as to deal with individual cases. By the beginning of 2002, over 1000 cases had been dealt with in this way (Roche 2003). Interestingly, although peace committees sit completely outside the formal criminal justice system, they do use it as a sword of Damocles in some cases. Roche (2003) describes a number of cases in which complainants were publicly offered help in bringing a formal complaint if the person whose behaviour was complained about did not fulfil the agreed conditions. However, informal solutions are often preferred: the example is given of a woman who complained to the peace committee that the agreement to return a stolen door to her had not been kept. The committee decided to reconvene the meeting, and the guilty party was asked to bring the door to the meeting with him!

The fees paid by the state for each case are divided between the central administration of the project (which supports the establishment of new committees and provides training and documentation) and the local committees. The peace committees, in turn, use a proportion of the money to remedy some of the problems underlying the disputes dealt with by the peace committees. South African townships have few community facilities, and peace committees have been able to finance significant improvements. Examples include building a children's playground, refurbishing an old people's home and providing loans to support small businesses selling food and clothing (Roche 2003). This was part of a deliberate strategy of empowering township residents both economically and in terms of building and sustaining community capacity for self-regulation (Braithwaite 2000).

This is a relatively modest initiative, but given the unpromising environment and its success to date, it seems a very promising one. It began as an action research project, and its progress has been well documented by Clifford Shearing (2001). It has already been replicated in Argentina. Like the Truth and Reconciliation Commission, despite all the flaws of that process, it has produced encouraging evidence that restorative justice can thrive in difficult circumstances and provide an inexpensive technology for breathing life into moribund criminal justice systems. The South African Law Commission has recommended its adaptation and use on a national basis (Roche 2003).

Potential benefits for victims: The evidence

The successful innovations described in the previous section suggest that restorative justice has considerable potential benefits for victims of crime if it is applied in the most favourable conditions. Where conditions are less congenial, it can often still provide victims with a better service than they might otherwise receive. However, restorative interventions have in many cases been designed by people who, for one reason or another, come to the task with a greater awareness of the needs of offenders than of victims' wishes and needs.

Some advocates of restorative justice have suggested that the benefits of such an approach vary according to how 'pure' the implementation of restorative principles is in each situation. They argue that there is a continuum running from 'fully restorative' to 'minimally restorative' or 'non-restorative' (see for example McCold 2000; van Ness 2002). While one might question the directness of the link between levels of restorativeness and benefits for participants (and which participants in particular benefit most from each model) the notion of a continuum offers a useful device for considering the potential benefits for victims. McCold argues that degrees of restorativeness are related to the extent to which the different stakeholders are actively involved in processes, and this makes a useful link to the discussion about the extent of victim participation and the level of such involvement that is necessary for credibility in victims' eyes.

By definition, restorative justice needs to involve at least offering victims a choice of becoming involved. Where this is not done properly, or is resourced inadequately, the claim to be implementing restorative justice is open to challenge. In the absence of the victim, according to McCold, interventions can only claim to be 'mostly restorative', and this description applies to sentencing circles, reparative boards and youth offender panels where victims are not involved, invited or represented (Crawford and Newburn 2003). To this extent, the typology is helpful in calling service providers to account: victims are unlikely to benefit from involvement if it is not adequately planned, facilitated or resourced.

Van Ness takes the argument further, suggesting that all parties need to meet, having been invited in a way that acknowledges their proper interests. Once involved, they must be treated respectfully, and the outcome should (at least) involve an apology and restitution. This would be the 'fully restorative' ideal, but it might not be achieved in all systems or cases, when lower degrees of restoration might be expected within a system which was nevertheless designed to be fully restorative. The obvious examples would be the family group conference attended by all parties, who have been adequately prepared, where an agreement satisfactory to each was reached and subsequently monitored and implemented, and the parties were successfully reconciled or reintegrated. As we have seen, evaluative research shows that successful fully restorative interventions are highly regarded by the victims who benefit from them.

Removal of one element would result in a 'moderately restorative system', and the failure to invite and acknowledge the interests of one party (either those of the offender, the victim or the wider community) is the most likely cause of this categorisation. Examples include shuttle mediation and victim awareness programmes with incarcerated offenders. Such schemes can be of great benefit to victims, but they might be more beneficial in many cases – where the parties desired it – if they had a greater restorative element.

Van Ness also proposes a 'minimally restorative system' which is the scenario in which there is a legitimate claim to being restorative in some way/s but without meeting more than one or two of the criteria he sets out. The system does not aspire to being fully restorative, and the interests of some parties are not systematically considered or provided for. Typically, this would cover systems which are mainly concerned with the material or financial costs of crime without aspiring to bring the parties together or even to hear all their views. Examples include compensation and victim support schemes. Clearly, these are enormously helpful to victims and only restorative to a certain extent.

Optimum conditions

While this typology of restorativeness offers some assistance in considering how helpful restorative justice can be to victims, a number of other issues also need to be considered. Thinking of criminal justice in restorative terms makes it clear that 'zero sum game' arguments are inappropriate: attacking the rights of offenders is unlikely to assist victims in the long term. While restorative justice does not offer a panacea, it does offer a more constructive way of looking at how best to deal with many crimes, and victims can benefit when state and other agencies overcome their adversarial attitudes towards one another. For example, the Referral Order in England and Wales has often brought people working with young offenders and those working with victims together, along with other interested parties, to consider appropriate ways in which reparation might be facilitated. This might involve a range of agencies which normally have no contact, or whose staff and volunteers are suspicious of one another, in working together in the interests of reconciling the needs of the victims, offenders and community.

A range of legal, constitutional and professional issues arises once agencies begin to implement restorative justice. These include issues of accountability, impartiality, fairness and proportionality, each of which is discussed at length in the literature. Suffice it to say that the rights of all parties must be genuinely respected; an appropriate balance between competing rights has to be struck; facilitators and service providers should ideally be impartial and be recognised as such by all parties; the legal framework should ensure that restorative disposals are dispensed fairly with due respect to proportionality and parsimony in sentencing. Given the evidence of unintended consequences in a number of jurisdictions, vigilance is required to ensure that implementation is effectively monitored in respect of gender, racial and other forms of discrimination and that appropriate action is taken on this information. (For further detail see Young and Goold 1999; Findlay 2000a and b; Miers 2001; Youth Justice Board for England and Wales 2001; Akester 2002; Braithwaite 2002; Strang 2002; Restorative Justice Consortium 2003; Home Office, Crown Prosecution Service and Department of Constitutional Affairs 2004; Tickell and Akester 2004.)

To be beneficial to victims, restorative interventions need to be individualised, not mechanistic. There is a real danger, when innovations are introduced, that they are added to the existing heavy workloads of criminal justice professionals and perceived as a burden: 'yet another new initiative to be managed as well as resources allow' (Tickell and Akester 2004, p.85). Unfortunately, this description of some youth justice practitioners' attitude towards reparation and referral orders is symptomatic of a wider issue. In the USA, the 'McDonaldization' of victim–offender mediation has been identified as a problem. Ill-prepared mediation meetings, undue emphasis on meeting performance targets and victims being routinely represented by professionals rather than being encouraged to take part in person can all combine to create 'fast-food mediation' (Umbreit 1999, p.226).

While there may be scope for some degree of standardisation, it is in the nature of restorative justice that it requires individual assessments of the needs and attitudes of participants, which take time. Too often in England and Wales since 1998, implementation has been rushed, resources have been scarce and innovation has been less restorative as a consequence. This is probably closely linked to the problem of low levels of victim participation, although there is no direct evidence of this. When these problems combine with a general reluctance to engage with victims, as has been the case in some youth offending teams, victims receive a poor service (Bailey and Williams 2000; Dignan 2002; Hoyle 2002; Masters 2002a; Restorative Justice Consortium 2003).

Changing the role of youth offender services to encompass services to victims is a massive cultural change which will require time and resources as well as staff training to implement successfully. One way of resisting such change – particularly when time, resources and training are lacking – has been to contract the work out to other organisations. Another is to cut corners by failing to consult victims sufficiently or at all (Dignan 2002). A third is to routinise reparation, requiring young people to undertake work in groups – an approach which bears little relation to the offence, the wishes of the victim or the young offenders' interests and abilities (Wilcox and Hoyle 2002). The emphasis upon numbers has tended to encourage this approach in the UK, which is very unfortunate. The result can be a sausage-machine, 'a form of junior community service with minimal reparative benefits' (Dignan 2000, p.24). It need not be this way, and practice in many areas is much more imaginative than this, but these dangers need to be carefully guarded against. The optimum conditions for restorative justice require an assessment process which is given sufficient time, and a repertoire of services and interventions which allows a creative choice between genuine alternatives for the parties concerned.

There is clearly a role for well-trained volunteers and sessional staff in ensuring that the parties are carefully prepared for their involvement in restorative justice. In a number of jurisdictions, this seems to be an important condition for success. This is reported to be a factor in relation to the successful implementation of Youth Offender Panels in England and Wales (Crawford and Newburn 2003); the introduction of community victim–offender mediation in Norway (Miers 2001; Tickell and Akester 2004) and, more recently, on an experimental basis in Denmark and Finland (Miers 2001), and the national victim assistance and mediation network in France. Volunteers may bring both legitimacy and a personal touch to such work, and they can also symbolise and personify community involvement in the justice system.

Restorative justice that meets victims' needs

In summary, restorative justice can meet victims' needs significantly better than conventional approaches if it is properly resourced and implemented, and if other necessary conditions are met.

Wemmers (2002) has helpfully summarised the research evidence on the potential benefits of restorative justice for victims. In terms of receiving information about the system and the offender, the picture is mixed. On the one hand, restorative approaches, as noted above, mean that victims are more likely to receive this information. On the other, restorative justice programme evaluations have consistently pointed to victim dissatisfaction in this area. Restorative programmes do not always do enough to pass on the information they have to victims.

In relation to compensation and restitution, restorative approaches have their strengths, but victims frequently complain that agreements reached with offenders are not effectively monitored or enforced. Nevertheless, it is probably the case that victims who take part in restorative interventions are more likely to receive some restitution than those in cases which go to court.

The emotional benefits of the best restorative justice programmes are well documented, and this is a major area of strength. Although victims of serious crime have a good deal to lose by becoming involved in face-to-face mediation, they also have the most to gain, and there are fairly consistent positive findings about this in the research.

The research evidence is somewhat ambiguous, and it is difficult to compare the results in different legal systems of varying practices which have been evaluated in inconsistent ways. Even the best restorative programmes can only work with the victims who come forward and the offenders who are apprehended, which is always likely to represent the tip of the iceberg. The research does suggest, however, that restorative justice offers considerable promise for dealing better with the wishes and needs of victims of crime, if it is properly resourced and if it adheres to the safeguards discussed in this chapter.

Chapter Four

Improving the position of victims of crime

This chapter begins by considering some of the conceptual difficulties involved in the project of attempting to 'rebalance' justice. It then gives further examples of changes in law and policies relating to victims of crime in a number of countries, and suggests some lessons which might be learnt from the experience of implementing these changes. In some cases, it appears that changes have been made without proper planning or consultation; in others changes appear to have been made mainly for presentational or political reasons and there are also examples of difficulties of implementation which might have been foreseen. While it is easy to be wise after the event, a comparative perspective can help to avoid the unnecessary costs involved in re-inventing the wheel and may serve to demonstrate that transferring policies and practices from one jurisdiction to another is not always advisable without at least piloting the initiative in the new setting first. In the process, victims' interests can be protected.

Some misunderstandings

One tendency common to a number of jurisdictions is to act against the interests of criminals and those accused of committing offences on the assumption that this is bound to be of assistance to victims. This has been identified as an issue particularly in the USA and in the UK. It has a number of elements, each identified in passing in earlier chapters of this book:

- Andrew Ashworth's 'victims in the service of severity' thesis, mentioned in Chapter One (Ashworth 2000), whereby victims of crime are called in aid of political arguments for harsher penal policies

- linked to this is the appropriation of concerns about victims to justify other policy initiatives which have little to do with victims' needs or interests, a problem first identified by Robert Elias in the USA in the 1980s (Elias 1984; Walklate 2004)

- the 'zero sum game' approach which gives rise to a belief in the necessity for 'rebalancing' justice to even out the power relations between the parties, as if there were a natural balance between provisions for victims and offenders which could be easily manipulated to ensure even-handedness (Hickman, 2004).

Victims in the service of severity

According to Ashworth (2000) and Garland (2001), victims have increasingly been used by politicians in an attempt to legitimise harsher approaches to sentencing offenders. In its crudest form, this has been seen in the use of crime victims at press conferences or party-political events announcing laws bringing in longer prison sentences or systems for notifying communities about the presence of ex-offenders in their midst. No attempt is made to engage in the complexities of debate about what would actually be best for communities or for victims: the strong feelings involved are taken as an indication that change is required and will prove beneficial.

An example of this at its worst is community notification schemes that were aimed at identifying sexual offenders returning to live in the community after prison sentences and which have simply led to the creation of more victims. US Federal law was amended in 1996 as a result of a campaign for 'Megan's law'. This was named after a seven-year-old girl who was sexually assaulted and murdered by a convicted sexual offender who lived in the same street as the girl and her family. Her mother campaigned internationally for the law to be changed, and in the US registers of sexual offenders which were already in place on a confidential basis were duly made public. There have been cases of vigilante activity in response to community notification, including beatings and arson (Doerner and Lab 2002), not always against the intended target (Freeman-Longo 2000). In England, a paediatrician was attacked by someone who did not understand that a paedophile was a different sort of person.

There is a danger that exceptional cases may be used to argue for extreme responses, especially in the kind of case where 'delivery of pain is seen as an instrument for the protection of the weak and vulnerable' (Christie 2004, p.37), and that fundamental rights can be forfeited in the process (Hudson 2004). The response to crime depends upon taking a moral position, not merely a political or pragmatic one. This can lead either to a defence of certain absolute rights for offenders, or to a situation in which victims are

> routinely invoked in support of measures of punitive segregation. In the USA politicians hold press conferences to announce mandatory sentencing laws and are accompanied at the podium by the family of crime victims. Laws are passed and named for victims: Megan's law, Jenna's law, the Brady bill. In the UK crime victims appear as featured speakers at political party conferences... (Garland 2001, p.11)

While there may be educational benefits for the audience and expressive benefits for the individual victims involved in such activities, there is bound to be a suspicion that politicians have less reputable motives in these cases. In these cases, the victim is not necessarily reflecting an existing demand of victims' organisations or the wishes of other victims: indeed, as Garland goes on to point out, what we know about victims' views from victimisation surveys suggests that these individuals may be entirely unrepresentative (and they may have been exploited at a time when they were most vulnerable).

The example of mandatory sentencing suggests that using victims 'in the service of severity' may prove counter-productive. Mandatory sentencing is likely, by definition, to lead to disproportionate penalties. It can produce extraordinary anomalies, such as the life sentence given out in California in 1995 for the theft of a slice of pizza. While mandatory sentencing laws in the UK include get-out clauses which should prevent such absurdities (Cavadino and Dignan 2002), injustices are nevertheless likely to occur from time to time. Offenders receiving such sentences are likely to be highly resentful, and even life-sentenced prisoners are eventually released in most countries. Bitterness is not conducive to rehabilitation or reformation, and these ex-prisoners are highly likely to re-offend, which cannot be in the interests of victims.

'Rebalancing' justice

> This sanctification of victims also tends to nullify concern for offenders. The zero sum relationship that is now assumed to hold between the one and the other ensures that any show of compassion for offenders, any

invocation of their rights, any effort to humanize their punishments, can easily be represented as an insult to victims and their families. (Garland 2001, p.143)

And yet, how punitive or vengeful are victims, and to what extent is it in their interests to pander to such attitudes where they exist? Many victims are less interested in revenge than in 'policies that really reduce victimization in the first place [and in…] influence, information, assistance, respect, remorse and accountability' (Elias 1993, p.117). Research has found 'no consistent evidence that experience of victimisation increases punitiveness' (Mayhew and van Kesteren 2002, p.77). Opinions about sentencing vary among victims in much the same way as they do among the wider public (Mattinson and Mirrlees-Black 2000). Public opinion favours the reform of offenders as well as their punishment (Doble 2002; Bottoms 2004), and there is some evidence that punitive attitudes decrease as people become better informed about sentencing (Hough and Park 2002).

Some efforts to alter the balance between victims' rights and those of offenders appear downright vindictive, the product of populist law-and-order politics. Elias (1993) gives a number of US examples, including the following:

- 'offenders are banned from being considered crime victims themselves' (p.31), which removes the right to compensation no matter how extreme the offences to which ex-offenders fall victim

- the removal in some states of the ban on illegally obtained evidence being used against defendants (p.31), which encourages misconduct by police and prosecuting authorities

- the removal of the presumption in favour of granting bail, resulting in a much greater likelihood that accused persons spend time in custody before they are tried (p.32).

Legal changes of a lesser degree have been made, and proposed, in the UK. Although compensation is not necessarily completely denied to ex-offenders, it is frequently reduced (see the discussion of compensation later in this chapter). A Home Office policy document, significantly entitled *Narrowing the Justice Gap*, has introduced targets for the proportion of prosecutions which result in convictions (Home Office 2002), an approach seen by some in the legal profession as an ominous precedent which creates 'perverse incentives for [the criminal justice system] to misbehave and convict the innocent' (Hickman 2004, p.56). The defendant's right to remain silent has been eroded. The government has proposed that criminal justice be speeded up by formalising the sentencing 'discounts' given in recognition of early guilty pleas, which some fear will make it more likely that innocent defendants are pressured to plead guilty (Jackson 2004). It is difficult to see any benefits for victims arising from these changes and proposals.

Whether compensation payments should be restricted because victims have previously offended is a matter for legitimate debate, but it is not an issue which is often raised, perhaps partly because of the common but erroneous assumption that victims and offenders are largely discrete groups which rarely overlap (Williams 1999a; Smith 2002; Muncie 2003). What is clear is that some victims are treated differently for reasons which they are likely to perceive as unfair, particularly if they regard themselves as having paid for their previous crimes and reformed their behaviour.

Changes to the criminal justice system which prejudice defendants' rights and increase the danger of unfair convictions are more obviously against victims' interests. If the wrong person is convicted of a crime, the true perpetrator remains undetected and is free to victimise others. Meanwhile, in more serious cases, innocent people can become bitter and destructive when imprisoned. There are, of course, wider issues involved: public confidence in the system is eroded when miscarriages of justice come to light, and some victims would be less inclined to report offences if they perceived a high likelihood of a wrongful conviction being the result. Tinkering with the legal rights of offenders, or deliberately reducing them, does not improve the lot of victims and may make it worse.

The rhetoric of 'rebalancing justice' has, however, been gaining ground in UK political discourse. The White Paper *Criminal Justice: The Way Ahead* (Home Office 2001) refers to such a balancing act and implies that the rights of one party are invariably achieved at the expense of another. The Prime Minister, interviewed about a forthcoming Criminal Justice Bill, used similar terminology, saying 'We will rebalance the system emphatically in favour of the victims of crime. Offenders get away too easily' (Ahmed 2002). Two years later, opposition leader Michael Howard employed the same image in similar circumstances, saying at an election rally:

> There is now a palpable sense of outrage that so-called human rights have tipped the balance of justice in favour of the criminal and the wrong-doer – rather than the victim and the law abider. (Watt 2004, p.4)

The notion that there is a natural equilibrium between victims' and offenders' rights which can be adjusted by making legal changes has, therefore, become quite entrenched despite its lack of any basis in reality.

The 'zero sum game'

A related fallacy is

> the assumption that a 'zero sum game' needs to be played whereby advancing the rights of defendants can lead only to losses for victims and, conversely, diminishing the rights and interests of the defence will automatically enure to the benefit of the prosecution. (Jackson 2004, p.66)

This goes beyond the idea of rebalancing the system to posit a fixed quantity of rights which can be distributed in a number of ways as between the parties, but cannot be increased or decreased. While it is clearly incorrect, given that rights can be created afresh and allocated to either or both parties in the criminal justice process, this concept has been influential in a number of jurisdictions. Elias (1993), for example, attributes the passage of a number of amendments to the US constitution to this way of thinking. It is important because it implies that victims' rights and treatment should be improved not as an end in itself, but as part of a wider reform which is believed inevitably to threaten the rights of others in the criminal process. Thus, a search for ways of achieving improvements in the treatment of victims tends to begin with an examination of the ways in which offenders are treated – once again falling into the trap of basing victim services and policies on needs revealed by those working with offenders (which is what most criminal lawyers specialise in doing). If victims and victims' organisations were consulted, it is unlikely that offenders' rights would be high on their agenda. Indeed, Victim Support in the UK has explicitly decided 'to avoid comment on offender related issues, other than those which directly affected victims or the development of services for them' (Reeves and Wright 1995, p.79).

Most of the examples given above of changes made or proposed to the treatment of offenders have no such direct impact upon victims, and to that extent they are largely irrelevant to a discussion of victims' rights and needs. The notion of 'rebalancing' justice against the interests of offenders and in favour of victims rests upon a false analogy.

Implementing change in the interests of victims

It is possible to make changes in the interests of victims of crime without relying upon a destructive polarisation between victims' interests and needs and those of the other parties involved. In practice, though, there is always likely to be a tension between straightforward implementation of changes to meet perceived needs and the realities of the political environment in which criminal justice issues are debated. The case studies which follow demonstrate some of the ways in which such tensions have been manifested in practice.

State-funded compensation schemes

In Chapter One, the place of state compensation for victims of crime in the history of services to victims was briefly outlined. In this section, some of the implementation issues are considered more fully.

The principles underlying compensation were always contested. Margery Fry saw it as a kind of social insurance, provided by the taxpayer in recognition of the fact that crime can impact upon anyone and a belief that victims should therefore be entitled to expect some recognition and support from the state. She described restitution as a principle well known to 'simple peoples' in earlier times, but one which had fallen into disuse in modern societies due to the bureaucratisation of the state (Fry 1951, p.124). For her and for the others who campaigned for compensation for victims, the schemes established to compensate the victims of violent and sexual crimes in a number of countries from 1963 represented an important, symbolic milestone and something of a moral victory. Political opponents, however, saw it as 'a political palliative', creating another unnecessary bureaucratic structure which was in danger of encouraging dependency and even reducing citizens' vigilance in avoiding victimisation (Meiners 1978, p.98; Black 1987). In the UK, it was made clear from the outset that the state was taking *responsibility* rather than accepting *liability*, and payments were described in the 1964 White Paper as *ex gratia* (made as a favour, rather than arising from a legal responsibility) for those deserving such support (Edelhertz and Geitz 1974). This was reiterated during the parliamentary debate on the legislation, when compensation was described as 'an expression of public sympathy' (Victim Support 2003, p.3). This was doubtless intended to undermine the claim that the social insurance principle created an entitlement to compensation, and the UK scheme has always been limited to victims of violent and sexual offences who are defined as 'innocent' (see below), although schemes in France and Finland now cover victims of property offences on a discretionary basis (CICP 1999).

It is mainly rich countries which have established state compensation schemes, and 'in jurisdictions where state compensation is most needed, no such schemes have been set up' (Brienen and Hoegen 2000, p.1162). Clearly, the least well-off victims of crime in the poorest countries have a greater need for compensation than most victims in rich countries. For example, the theft of a bicycle would be regarded as a mere inconvenience in many cases in a European context, whereas it could threaten the victim's livelihood if it happened in parts of Africa (where it is a frequent occurrence and is generally regarded as a serious offence, as noted in the findings of the International Crime Victimisation Survey – see Prinsloo *et al.* 2001). Similarly, the costs incurred by assault victims, including lost earnings, take on greater significance in countries without extensive free health and welfare provision, but these are the very countries which are least likely to be able to afford generous – or any – state compensation arrangements.

Although the first compensation scheme, in New Zealand, placed state compensation to victims of crime on the same footing as the compensation paid to those involved in industrial accidents or car accidents (Black 1987; CICP 1999), the UK scheme was more circumscribed from the start. It was never intended to cover the victims of corporate crimes (Dignan 2005) and it made a distinction between deserving and undeserving victims which has had a continuing influence upon practice in other jurisdictions as well as creating anomalies in decision-making which cause considerable distress to individual victims. Indeed, Victim Support has described some aspects of the administration of the scheme as constituting a form of re-victimisation (Victim Support 2003, p.3).

The notion of distinguishing between deserving and undeserving victims reflects the thinking of the time: this was conventional wisdom even among victimologists until much more recently (Williams 1999a). It has been refined to a certain extent in almost half a century's experience of administering state compensation, but it has also been institutionalised in the compensation arrangements in a number of countries. The Council of Europe agreed a Convention on the Compensation of Victims of Violent Crimes in 1988 which suggested that compensation should only be payable to victims who were innocent of criminal activity and 'contributory misconduct' (CICP 1999, p.45). This reflects practice in the UK, where victims normally have to show that they reported an offence promptly and co-operated fully with the police; were not themselves to blame for what happened, did not cohabit with the offender and do not have prior, unspent, serious criminal convictions (CICA

2001). The compensation authority's guidance to claimants explains this as follows:

> a person who has committed criminal offences has probably caused distress and loss and injury to other persons, and has certainly caused considerable expense to society by reason of court appearances and the cost of supervising sentences, even when they have been non-custodial, and the victims may themselves have sought compensation, which is another charge on society. Even though an applicant may be blameless in the incident in which the injury was sustained, parliament has provided in the Scheme that convictions which are not spent under the Rehabilitation of Offenders Act 1974 should be taken into account. (CICA 2001, p.14)

The practical effect of the section on unspent offences is that anyone who is serving or has served a prison sentence is disqualified from receiving compensation for a number of years after their release (up to 10) or has compensation rates reduced by a fixed percentage depending on how much time has passed. This comes as a surprise to would-be claimants, particularly in cases where a murder victim's children are disqualified from receiving compensation in other cases because the victim had a criminal record (Victim Support 2003, p.10).

Victim Support has drawn attention to a number of other anomalies. Compensation payments are treated as capital for the purpose of calculating means-tested benefits, which means that in many cases successful claimants' benefits payments are reduced to reflect their success in claiming compensation. The rules do not define a crime of violence, and in practice this has led to many sexual abuse victims being disqualified on the grounds that it was impossible to ascertain whether or not they had consented to sexual assaults within the home. Naturally, this is extremely upsetting for the claimants concerned, many of whom will have been groomed for victimisation over a period of time rather than being physically coerced:

> the rejection could lead to people feeling that they are not seen as worthy of society's sympathy... Many victims will already feel guilty, as if they are to blame in some way. Victim Support believes that the refusal of an award on these grounds will look like confirmation of their guilt. This is the complete opposite of the message that the scheme was set up to send out. (Victim Support 2003, p.4)

However, an alternative way of viewing these rules and the way in which they have been interpreted is that this discrimination in fact reflects the intentions of the original legislation in that it differentiates between victims who are seen as deserving public sympathy and those who are regarded as somehow tainted by their situation. Benefit claimants, the children of people who have served prison sentences and the survivors of child sexual abuse are the subjects of the discretion which was deliberately built into the scheme. As the Victim Support pamphlet concludes,

> Compensation has an important role in demonstrating that society cares about what has happened. But the scheme compounds – not helps – the harm caused to someone if it denies a compensation award on the grounds that they do not deserve it (i.e. because of the type of crime, or if they were living with the offender. (Victim Support 2003, p.11)

Victim Support has chosen to highlight particular anomalies which are likely to command public support – not surprisingly, since it is a campaigning organisation aiming to achieve better results for the majority of victims. No real challenge has been mounted, however, to the principles of discretionary payment or of the concept of deservingness in general. If the scheme were to be reconstituted without these judgemental elements, the rationale for denying compensation to certain people with criminal convictions would also fall (and every change of this kind has cost implications). Interestingly, the decision to move from an almost completely discretionary scheme to one based on a 'tariff' was criticised at the time for potential unfairness and for being aimed at cutting the cost of the scheme, but it too has become increasingly costly despite being poorly publicised. It paid out £160m in 2003 (Williams 1999a; Home Office 2004a). The most recent review of the compensation scheme (Home Office 2004c) side-steps this issue: the summary of responses to a consultation notes that

> Several respondents commented that compensation payments to victims should come from a central fund with offenders making payments to the fund rather than in piecemeal instalments to the victim. This would assist victims with 'closure' of the incident that led to their victimisation... (Home Office 2004c, p.8)

The paragraph which follows the one quoted outlines the government's intentions, but makes no reference to the preceding comments.

Compensation paid by the offender

Surcharging offenders to pay for victim services began in the USA with the establishment of a Crime Victims Fund under the 1984 Federal Victims of Crime Act. The fund receives most of its income directly from offenders and redistributes the money to victim services and individual victims in a variety of ways (although this source of funding is not well known and take-up by individuals is poor) (Doerner and Lab 2002). The UK government has introduced a similar scheme based upon surcharges on fines and fixed penalty notices, operating a sliding scale according to the size of the original penalty, despite widespread opposition to the idea during a consultation period and in both houses of parliament.[1] As well as what might be regarded as predictable and partisan opposition from certain quarters, the idea was also opposed in principle by police and magistrates' organisations and some judges (Hansard 2004). The legislation goes further than originally proposed, allowing the Criminal Injuries Compensation Authority to recover from offenders the state compensation paid to victims in some circumstances (Domestic Violence, Crime and Victims Act 2004, section 57). The money will then be distributed from the centrally held Victims' Fund, both to compensate individuals and to fund victims' organisations (Home Office 2004b).

The principle of surcharging offenders has been established in the USA for 20 years, and it no longer appears to be controversial there (Doerner and Lab 2002). However, its public acceptability in the UK will depend upon how it is implemented in practice. There was a widespread belief, expressed during the consultation period and in the parliamentary debates on the legislation, that it would create unfairness (and some newspaper editorials – along with the Magistrates' Association – described it as 'a further hidden tax on motorists'; see Hansard 2004, column 1499). The government responded to some of these criticisms by reducing the scope of the law in relation to motoring offences and by saying that the operation of the scheme would be subject to review by the Commissioner for Victims and Witnesses, a new post created by the same piece of legislation.

Compensation levied by courts upon offenders as a sentence (or part of one) is also important both symbolically and practically to many victims.

---

1   Vocal opposition by the motoring lobby and the insurance industry led to the amendment of the original proposals in order to omit 'ordinary' motoring offenders from the arrangements: they apply only to 'the most serious and persistent offenders' where motoring is concerned (Home Office 2004b).

It shows official disapproval of the offence, but also recognition of the victim's loss, and it holds the offender accountable in a tangible way. Unfortunately, it is subject to a number of implementation problems. Compensation has been available as a penalty in England and Wales since 1972, but courts do not always remember to consider ordering compensation (even though they have been required to do so in appropriate cases since s. 104 of the Criminal Justice Act 1988 came into force[2]). In many cases, courts are reluctant to order compensation due to offenders' poverty and the impossibility of ordering the payment of realistic amounts, or because they have insufficient objective information about the offender's means (see Cavadino and Dignan 2002, pp.132–4). In an era of increased use of prison sentences, courts are correspondingly unlikely to order offenders to pay compensation to victims, since most imprisoned offenders have hardly any financial resources. The number of compensation orders given in England and Wales declined steadily from the early 1990s at a time when the use of custodial sentences was increasing correspondingly (Dignan 2005, pp.80–1).

Even when courts do order offenders to pay compensation, enforcement is often problematic: compensation may be received by victims in very small instalments, if at all, and this may be perceived as insulting or as trivialising the original offence, as well as serving as a periodic reminder of the loss involved. This is particularly likely to occur in those cases where courts combine fines with compensation orders where the offenders have limited means (Dignan 2005).

Compensation is now collected and paid before fines and costs in England and Wales, in Scotland and in Spain, but this is not the case elsewhere (Brienen and Hoegen 2000). Nowhere in Europe has an 'up-front' payment system been introduced (that is, a system in which the state pays compensation to the victim and then, subsequently, recovers it from the offender), for the obvious reason that this would involve a substantial and unpredictable increase in public expenditure (Justice 1998; CICP 1999; Cavadino and Dignan 2002). The government in England and Wales has, however, agreed to 'consider' introducing such a system (Home Office 2001, para. 3.118) and to improve enforcement procedures (Home Office 2004c). In The Netherlands, the responsibility for collecting compensation is passed on from the

---

2   Subsequently consolidated in ss. 130–4 of the 2000 Powers of the Criminal Courts (Sentencing) Act.

courts to the public prosecutor in cases where the offender is also placed under statutory supervision, and this improves repayment rates. Elsewhere, however, as in Malta and Germany, the probation service is given this task and fails to fulfil it satisfactorily. In Norway and Sweden there is a state debt recovery agency which has the collection of compensation as one of its responsibilities, and this is very successful. Recovery rates in the UK are widely regarded as low, but they seem to be high by international standards, although lower than in Norway and Sweden (Brienen and Hoegen 2000). It is difficult to envisage how the Norwegian or Swedish model would fit into the very different legal systems in other countries, but the principle of state responsibility for the collection of compensation is already well established in a number of countries: the problem is one of effective enforcement. Much might be learnt from Scandinavian successes in this area.

In the USA, compensation is called 'restitution', a term which confusingly also covers unpaid work for the victim or the community. The extent to which it is used there depends upon state laws which in turn vary according to the degree of willingness to spend the money required to make arrangements for collecting and distributing compensation. Since 1984, Federal legislation has provided for state funding for medical and psychiatric treatment costs incurred by crime victims, and for compensation to the survivors of murder victims. In addition, anyone injured or killed in the course of trying to prevent a crime is eligible for compensation – the so-called 'Good Samaritan provisions' (Doerner and Lab 2002). The Federal funding is largely drawn from money seized from offenders but, once the Federal scheme was set up, there were incentives for lawyers to offer to fight cases for victims on a 'no win, no fee' basis, which may have encouraged an increase in claims for compensation (Meiners 1978). In France, a levy is added to each personal insurance policy towards the funding of the state compensation programme, an effective tax on those better able to afford to protect themselves (CICP 1999).

Although European jurisdictions which have ratified it are bound by the Council of Europe Recommendation on the Position of the Victim in the Framework of Criminal Law and Procedure, implementation of the provisions on compensation is generally poor (Brienen and Hoegen 2000, p.1099; Goodey 2005). Compensation orders are a relative success story, in that they are better enforced and they are made more frequently than other legal mechanisms for compensating victims. However, one fifth of victims in England and Wales who are led to believe that they will receive compensation through the making of such an order still do not receive it, and it is not considered by the courts in all relevant cases despite the legal requirement that it should be.

This is a regrettable example of a law, passed for victims' benefit, which is not consistently implemented.

Victim Impact Statements

First introduced in the USA in the mid-1970s and in Canada in the late 1980s, Victim Impact Statements (VIS) were intended to improve victims' position within the criminal justice system by creating an opportunity for them to give information about the loss and the physical and emotional damage that they had suffered as a result of the offence, and to express their feelings about this. Not only would this involve victims more visibly in a system which had traditionally marginalised them (and it might thus to some extent empower them and give them a more dignified role), it was also intended to have an impact upon the culture of the system by allowing case-hardened practitioners to obtain a victim perspective. Judges, lawyers and others making decisions about cases would have access to victims' views more systematically than in the past, and this was expected to inform their decision-making.

In the USA, the use of VIS ran into constitutional problems from a fairly early stage, because emotive victim statements were being read to courts even in potentially capital cases, and inflaming emotions in a way which made decision-making more difficult. As a result, the higher courts ordered restrictions on the use of the statements in the most serious cases[3] – which also happened for different reasons in the UK, where the Lord Chief Justice urged judges to distinguish between victims' *losses* and their *opinions*: the former should be taken into account, but not the latter. The Court of Appeal later revisited this decision, and ruled that victims' opinions could be taken into account in certain circumstances, such as when they appealed for leniency and a particular sentence would be likely to increase their distress, or when an appeal for leniency showed that they were less distressed than might be expected in the circumstances of the case (Doerner and Lab 2002; Edwards 2002; Zedner 2002). This ruling on the link between forgiveness and mitigation raised more questions than it answered (see below).

---

3   Restrictions were introduced after the Booth *versus* Maryland case in 1987 on the grounds that VIS in capital cases threatened the Eighth Amendment prohibition on cruel and unusual punishment. This decision was overturned in 1991 in Payne *versus* Tennessee, which ruled that both VIS and victim allocution (verbal evidence) were constitutional (see Arrigo and Williams 2003).

Some observers argued that the legal profession was resistant to change on principle, and that many of the objections to VIS originated from prejudice and an unwillingness to give the reform a chance (Erez 2004). Legal concerns included the danger that victims might be further distressed by being called to give evidence to substantiate statements made in VIS which were challenged by defence lawyers (not, in practice, a frequent occurrence because the defence usually avoids antagonising judges and juries in this way) and a concern that VIS would introduce an additional element of inconsistency into proceedings by drawing the attention of sentencers to unforeseen harm done by offenders in particular cases where a VIS happened to have been prepared (Ashworth 1993). In Canada, Abramovsky (1992) argues that VIS increase inconsistency because they allow sentences to be influenced by the eloquence and social standing of the victim, which are irrelevant factors.

The possible benefits of VIS include empowering victims to have their views and concerns taken into account, which can enhance their feelings of dignity and self-worth and their confidence in the criminal justice system. For some victims, the process helps to facilitate 'closure'; that is, it makes it easier for victims to put the incident behind them (Hinton 1995; Wemmers 1996; Erez 1999). The VIS process can also facilitate the claiming of compensation by ensuring that the court has accurate information about the extent of victims' losses. Up-to-date VIS can assist courts in reaching appropriate sentencing decisions in the light of all the facts, and this may be reflected in judges' comments when summing up: 'victims feel gratified when their sense of harm is validated in judges' remarks' (Erez 1999, p.553). Judges find the information helpful in at least some cases: a study in Ontario found that nearly half of the sample of Canadian judges said they found VIS useful in most or all cases where they were available, and more than half (52%) said that VIS sometimes contained relevant information that had not emerged from any other source during a case (Roberts and Edgar 2003). A US study showed that judges particularly valued the opportunity to receive information on financial losses and physical and psychological harm suffered by victims (Hillenbrand and Smith 1989, cited in Ashworth 1993).

The availability of VIS, even in a minority of cases, can improve the understanding and sensitivity of criminal justice professionals by apprising them of the effects of victimisation (Erez and Rogers 1999; Davis *et al.* 2002). Successful involvement in the VIS process should increase victims' likelihood of co-operating with the criminal justice system and have an impact upon public views on the legitimacy of the criminal justice system as a whole (Wemmers 1996; Walklate 2002).

Take-up rates of VIS were relatively low among victims in the USA and, later, elsewhere; far fewer statements were made than expected, although it was initially unclear what reasons lay behind this (Hoyle *et al.* 1999; Doerner and Lab 2002; Roberts and Edgar 2003). In the USA, about 15 per cent of the victims invited to submit written VIS do so; an additional 9 per cent take up the opportunity to present oral statements in those states where this is permitted. In Canada, about 15 per cent of victims take up the offer of making a written statement (JHSA 1997). Possible explanations for low take-up in the early days included difficulty in tracing victims, failure to inform them of their right to make a statement, and victims choosing, for a variety of reasons, not to take part. Research established that these were all valid reasons, and that the range of causes of victims declining to participate included fear of retaliation by offenders, general dissatisfaction with and distrust of the criminal justice system, a disinclination to expose themselves to further emotional distress, a desire to put the offence behind them and get on with life and a feeling that the matter was not serious enough to justify making a statement (Erez and Tontodonata 1992; Hoyle *et al.* 1999). There was also a belief on the part of some participants that no notice would be taken of whatever they said, a feeling also observed when Victim Personal Statements were piloted in England (Hoyle *et al.* 1999). It was, to some extent, borne out in practice (an issue discussed further below).

There was considerable controversy among researchers and practitioners in various countries about the extent to which participating in the VIS process made victims feel any better or made judges feel better informed (Gilberti 1991; Sanders *et al.* 2001; Roberts and Edgar 2003), and low levels of participation made the argument that VIS empowered victims ring somewhat hollow. The pilot project in England involved a modified version of VIS, re-named Victim Personal Statements, which aimed to avoid some of the disadvantages of the US model. It explicitly avoided canvassing victims' views about sentencing and made it clear that VPS would not normally be taken into account after a finding of guilt; it also provided that VPS would be disclosed routinely to the defence (Home Office undated). The VIS has been adapted from the US model or emulated in a number of jurisdictions, including Australia, Canada, Ireland, The Netherlands and Scotland.

Some authors have suggested that US politicians introduced VIS primarily for political reasons – to show that 'something was being done' for victims (Ashworth 2000; Garland 2001). Given the ambiguity of the research evidence briefly reviewed above, it does seem difficult otherwise to explain the enthusiasm of legislators in other jurisdictions for undertaking similar experiments in their own countries. While it is true that (for example in Ireland, England and Wales and Scotland) these VIS schemes were explicitly designed to avoid some of the pitfalls observed in the US, they all derive from the same principles and they are likely to face at least some of the same problems (Walklate 2002). New ideas spread rapidly in criminal justice, and politicians do not always take sufficient (or any) notice of research evidence. The careful, measured evaluation of the pilot VIS scheme in England and Wales by Hoyle *et al.* (1999) in which evidence for not introducing VIS in England and Wales was provided, was swiftly followed by the Home Office decision to 'roll out' Victim Personal Statements nationally, and the authors became somewhat more impassioned in their subsequent discussions of the issues (Sanders *et al.* 2001). They are not the only observers to have suggested that more evidence is required that VPS do not merely raise victims' expectations unrealistically without providing tangible benefits in many cases (see for example Goodey 2000; Edwards 2002; Walklate 2002).

One of the reasons some victims gave for refusing to provide VPS was that they did not believe that their views would actually be taken into account. There is some evidence that their concerns were justified, at least in England and Wales and possibly in Australia. According to an early piece of research on the UK pilot projects, some VPS were withheld by the Crown Prosecution Service if they were not felt to add anything to the evidence, and not all prosecutors made them available to the defence. Many prosecutors saw VPS merely as background material for their own evidence, and neither the court nor the victim and witnesses would be aware that this was the source of the information given in court. The researchers found that statements

> seldom influence sentencing decisions in any direction. Nonetheless, it is *only* in relation to sentencing that VSs have any significant effect. This is ironic, given the belief and hope of many advocates of victim involvement in the UK that VSs should primarily influence earlier decisions… (Morgan and Sanders 1999, p.18, emphasis in the original)

It should be noted, though, that this was in the early days of the pilot projects, and many of the legal professionals interviewed had seen few, if any, Victim Personal Statements. Although take-up continued to be low when the VPS scheme was made available nationally, it may well have increased since 2001. This will become clearer when an evaluation of the scheme is completed by the Office for Criminal Justice Reform (an inter-departmental body based in the Home Office) in 2005. An evaluation study in South Australia found that 34 per cent of victims who prepared a VIS felt that it did not have the impact upon sentencing that they expected (Hinton 1995). In the UK, however, it is routinely made clear to victims that this is not the intention of the statement scheme.

It is possible that VPS were seen as 'a good idea' despite the lack of evidence that many victims benefited from them, because there were other reasons to introduce them. There is a body of opinion suggesting that the initiative was, in fact, primarily a political one, not driven mainly by victims' needs or wishes. Members of the pilot projects' evaluation team have been particularly vocal on this issue, but others have also added their voices. For example,

> VSs are supported by most decision-makers [judges and lawyers] at the level of rhetoric but not at the level of action. (Morgan and Sanders 1999, p.23)

> The best way forward is to improve victim services rather than rely on new procedural rights for victims. The right to submit a VIS may be high in profile but low in improving genuine respect for victims. (Ashworth 1993, quoted in Sanders *et al.* 2001, p.449)

> any reform for victims should be aimed at *actually* benefiting them practically rather than being, as Jo Goodey describes victim impact statements, 'a mute political gesture to appease certain victims and victim lobby groups'. (Edwards 2002, pp.701–2)

> If the major reason why most victims in conventional adversarial systems feel marginalised is that they give one (witness) statement and are then ignored, why should VIS – in which they give two statements and are then ignored – make any difference? ...Confronted on TV with the findings of Hoyle *et al.*, the responsible government minister repeated the mantra that 'this is what victims want', deliberately ignoring the point that many wanted them only before they were made and then ignored. (Sanders 2004, pp.102–3)

An appeal case in 1999 was briefly mentioned above, and it merits further discussion. In it, a driver pleaded guilty to causing death by careless driving while under the influence of drugs or drink. The person killed was the driver's cousin, who was a passenger in the car. The victim's mother and the prisoner's mother (who were sisters) both wrote to the court asking that the sentence be reduced because it was delaying their grieving processes. Lord Bingham ruled that, while neither a victim's desire for vengeance nor their desire for compassion should normally influence sentencing, this was a special case. He reduced the sentence from four years' imprisonment to three, arguing that it was sometimes appropriate for courts to exercise compassion in the light of appeals for mercy (Edwards 2002). In doing so, he chose to ignore the Lord Chief Justice's practice direction which explicitly makes clear that 'The opinions of the victim or the victim's close relative as to what the sentence should be are...not relevant' (quoted in Edwards 2002, p.691). As Edwards points out, this leaves the role of victims' views in need of clarification. Do victims have a say in defining the public interest in specific cases? Does forgiveness have a place in sentencing? Victims completing VPS are told that their views on sentencing are not sought and that what the court wants to know is how the offence has affected them – but it appears that case law may have changed this position, and that it may change further in the future.

Victim statements are a controversial measure and the controversy has continued over a lengthy period in several jurisdictions. To some extent, the problem seems to be that a primarily bureaucratic process is described by its advocates as enhancing victims' dignity and empowering them, when only a minority of victims seem interested in making use of it. It is quite possible that an administrative measure can enhance victims' dignity and help them achieve closure, but it is, by definition, not tailored to meet individual needs. Those victims who do give statements mostly say that they find the process useful. However, a significant minority do not, and many of them suspect that their opinions are not taken seriously. The research evidence is confusing, partly because much of it is so passionately argued. Although they are firmly in the 'anti' camp, Sanders and colleagues are undoubtedly right when they identify one problem with VIS: they say that

> The general message from our research, and the experience in other jurisdictions, is that schemes that provide information to victims without interaction and discussion with them do not in themselves increase satisfaction with the criminal justice system. (Sanders *et al.* 2001, p.452)

As we shall see, this message applies more broadly than simply to Victim Impact or Personal Statements.

Victim contact teams

There is a good deal of research evidence that victims of crime benefit from being kept informed about the progress of the criminal cases in which they are involved, and that failure to provide this information can make life more difficult for them. Wanting to be kept informed is one of the most significant needs identified by victims of crime (Mawby and Walklate 1994; Tudor 2002). Since the early 1990s, the probation service in England and Wales has been responsible for giving victims of more serious crime a choice about whether they wish to be kept informed about the outcomes of their cases and, where an offender is sentenced to custody, providing information about the subsequent treatment and eventual release of the person concerned. Since 2000, this has applied to all cases in which the offender is sentenced to imprisonment for 12 months or more, and after some teething problems the requirement is now being implemented successfully in the great majority of cases (Her Majesty's Inspectorate of Probation 2003). Many probation areas also offer the service to victims in sensitive cases such as racially motivated crime regardless of the sentence passed on the offender. Particularly where the shorter sentences are concerned, rates of take-up of the offer of information are low, however – and male victims are much less likely to make contact with the probation service than their female counterparts. Fewer than 40 per cent of victims take up the service, although this increases to a little over 50 per cent in the case of sexual offences, according to one study (Newton 2003). It seems likely that victims' attitudes towards the probation service, which remains primarily concerned with the supervision and surveillance of offenders, are a key factor in this low response. Being kept informed is, after all, something which victims consistently demand when asked about their expectations of the criminal justice system (Maguire and Kynch 2000, p.9; Justice 1998; Hoyle *et al.* 1999).

In other jurisdictions, the problem has been approached in a range of other ways. In The Netherlands, for example, the police were given this role and it is clear that when they implement the policy which requires them to keep victims informed, this increases victims' overall satisfaction with the criminal justice system. Sadly, implementation is inconsistent and according to several research studies in the 1990s, fewer than 40 per cent of those entitled to information were actually provided with it (Wemmers 1996). More recently, the Dutch police have begun to work alongside victim support agencies to ensure that victims are kept informed. Victims of serious offences are also invited to meet the prosecutor to express any concerns they may have about their cases (Brienen and Hoegen 2000).

In France, the authorities have published a *Victim's Guide*, available in court buildings, and the responsibility for keeping victims informed about their cases has been formally handed over to voluntary victim support agencies. However, there appears to be no national system for ensuring that the police pass on referrals to the relevant services, with the result that there is considerable local variation. Prosecutors are legally required to keep civil claimants (which includes many victims) informed of developments in cases, including the outcomes of police investigations and decisions to drop cases. In Sweden, victims of serious sexual and violent offences are entitled to legal aid to assist them in obtaining their rights (although take-up is low, perhaps due to a failure by the police and prosecution services to inform them of this right) (Brienen and Hoegen 2000).

Victim satisfaction with their treatment is likely to be adversely affected by offers of help which does not actually materialise, and this is clearly the case when the police offer to keep people informed and then fail to follow this through in practice, as frequently occurs in a number of countries including Scotland (Curry *et al.* 2004).

Overall, across the world, the issue of how best to keep victims informed remains unresolved. Examples above come from Europe because the Council of Europe Recommendation provides such a comprehensive guide to good practice, and Brienen and Hoegen's research (2000) gives a valuable snapshot of the extent to which is has been implemented and the kind of constraints which have prevented full achievement of its aspirations. It also shows how different the criminal justice systems are from one country to another, and how an apparently simple problem needs to be solved in radically different ways according to the kind of system concerned.

On the face of it, the decision in England and Wales to give the responsibility for keeping more serious victims informed to the probation service was an idiosyncratic one (and it seems to be a unique system). It raised issues about the ability of probation staff, accustomed to working primarily with offenders, to maintain objectivity and gain the confidence of victims. It also raised concerns that victims might be unwillingly drawn into involvement in decisions about offenders which should properly be taken elsewhere. It was introduced by central government without consultation and, initially, without additional resources, and it is therefore hardly surprising that it took some time for a service to be made available to victims consistently around the country (see Williams 1999, 1999a; Tudor 2002). The probation service had a number of attributes which made it capable of taking on the work: it had a long-standing relationship with most of the voluntary victim support agencies, it worked routinely with the police and prison services and it employed social work trained staff who could be expected to cope with the emotional needs of victims of serious crime. It was also in danger of being restructured or even abolished by the then government, so it was unlikely to raise strenuous objections to being given additional work without extra resources, and it was nowhere near as influential as the police and prison services. The other agency which might have been allocated the work was the prosecution service, but at the time the CPS was understaffed, disorganised and demoralised, and allocating extra, highly sensitive work to it would have been risky.

Regardless of the background to the introduction of victim contact work within probation, it has had a considerable impact upon the nature of the service offered to victims. Probation services have recognised the inconsistencies built into a system based on the sentences the offenders happen to receive by extending the victim contact role beyond what is legally required, although regional variations still remain. The teething problems in the early 1990s also meant that a variety of different ways of providing the service emerged, with some areas operating in close partnership with Victim Support schemes and giving a good deal of time to interviews with victims, while others initially perceived the service as a largely bureaucratic exchange of information and tried to dissuade staff from becoming involved with victims' problems (Crawford and Enterkin 1999; Tudor 2002). The latter approach was problematic for victims – particularly those seriously affected by the crime – because it failed to recognise some people's need to ventilate their emotions, sometimes at length. Probation workers who attempted to remain emotionally detached were in danger of giving offence and even revictimising the people they were there to help. It would appear, however, that ways have since been found of avoiding these dangers.

Victims are contacted either at court or soon afterwards, with the offer of information and continuing contact. It is made clear to them that the service is provided in order to improve the flow of information and to ensure that the victim's concerns are heard. Despite some reservations about hearing from the probation service, which is widely perceived as an organisation dedicated mainly to working with offenders, many victims welcome receiving the service from a professional rather than a voluntary agency, and victims' levels of satisfaction with the service received are high (Crawford and Enterkin 1999; Her Majesty's Inspectorate of Probation 2003). Victim contact workers explain to victims how the criminal justice system operates, and talk them through the implications of providing information to prisons and the parole board in cases where offenders are being considered for early release. Victims have the opportunity to make representations about parole conditions in serious cases and this can provide considerable reassurance: prisoners can be conditionally released without necessarily being aware that the conditions have been imposed in response to victims' concerns. While there is a danger of asking questions years after an offence and thus reopening issues which the victims would prefer to put behind them, a sensitive worker can help victims resolve such issues. In appropriate cases, victims are referred on to other agencies for additional help. The service is provided to victims of the most serious offences, as well as to the bereaved in murder cases, and some victims display high levels of need. Where they need to tell and re-tell their stories, this is not a role the probation staff can take on, and they therefore make referrals to specialist agencies.

Two inspections of probation service work with victims have highlighted deficiencies in the service, particularly relating to staff training, diversity issues and liaison with other agencies in relation to child victims. Local areas have responded by further developing their work in these areas, particularly in ensuring that victim services are accessible to all and that the relevant staff receive appropriate and on-going training. Victims' organisations and researchers in the area have been consulted and involved in the formulation of policy, and the quality of services is monitored in a variety of ways (see for example Leicestershire and Rutland Probation Area 2004).

The development of this service has also enabled probation staff to work in more sophisticated ways with offenders around victim issues, although this is a spin-off rather than a central task for victim contact staff. It is relevant to victims' interests, however, insofar as it may help to prevent future victimisation by sensitising offenders to victims' feelings and ensuring that probation officers supervising offenders have accurate information, wherever possible, about the impact of offences upon victims. This makes collusion with offenders' excuses much less likely and it is likely to lead to more victim-sensitive decision-making when the question of the offender's release on parole or licence arises. In many cases, contact with victims provides a completely different perspective on cases where the offender has rationalised or denied aspects of their offending.

The main improvements from victims' point of view concern being kept informed, having an opportunity to influence decision-making and, in some cases, receiving appropriate protection. There are limits to the information provided to victims, not least because of a concern about the possibility that some would take revenge if they had detailed information about offenders' plans after release from prison, but most victims can understand the reasoning behind this policy.

A number of lessons can be learnt from the experience of implementing victim contact. An obvious one is that it is unwise to do things 'for' victims without consultation. The initial implementation problems arose largely from the then government's failure to find out what victims wanted before introducing the service. This was compounded by the lack of new resources to introduce the victim contact arrangements, which meant that it was several years before a consistent service emerged. Once the probation service found ways of monitoring the effectiveness of its victim contact arrangements, improvements were rapidly made (in response, for example, to the findings of the two thematic inspections undertaken by Her Majesty's Inspectorate of Probation, but also to surveys by opinion poll companies and internal victim surveys by individual probation areas).

Different models of victim support

The type and extent of service provision for victims of crime varies enormously between countries, as Mawby (2003) has shown. In the USA there is a strong emphasis on providing victims with professional counselling; in contrast to the self-help model which prevails in western Europe, where volunteers are more likely to be deployed to provide neighbourly support to victims and refer particular cases on to professional services where required. In the UK, Victim Support gave priority to the victims of property offences for many years, perhaps because this was the most frequent type of offending and the easiest for volunteers to deal with, while North American victim agencies concentrated upon victims of violent offences. Victim Support now provides different levels of training to its volunteers, and there are many who are able to support victims of serious violent offences. Specialist organisations such as Support After Murder and Manslaughter, Rape Crisis and Women's Aid have also developed alongside Victim Support and offer long-term support. Their funding is often insecure, however, and this makes it very difficult for them to provide more than skeleton services in many cases. The struggle to obtain the necessary funding adds further pressure to the demanding jobs of staff and volunteers in such agencies, and the service to victims can be compromised as a result (see Chapter Six).

In The Netherlands, services to support victims were originally set up by the probation service, and there has always been a strong emphasis upon victim–offender mediation (which is viewed with suspicion by victim advocates in many other countries) and on referral to professional counselling agencies (which is beyond the resources of services in other jurisdictions). The Dutch victim support arrangements have always covered victims of road traffic accidents, while in England and Wales this has not formally been the case – although extending services to such victims is now under discussion here, and local schemes have always exercised some discretion in this matter.

While victim support services in countries such as The Netherlands, England and Wales, and Scotland are provided on a national, fairly standardised basis, this is far from being the case in countries with federal systems such as the USA or Belgium. In other jurisdictions such as Germany and most eastern European countries, provision is much patchier, depending upon locally available resources. German victim support agencies tend to concentrate upon providing legal and financial help rather than emotional support. Services for victims are generally not well developed in countries with no tradition of voluntary activity by non-governmental organisations, such as South Africa or some eastern European countries. Engagement with the victims of more serious crimes is the exception rather than the norm internationally, and appears to be at its most sophisticated in western Europe and North America – which is to say, in the richer countries – although it has also developed in response to unmet need in countries in violent transition such as South Africa and Northern Ireland.

To some extent, the varying models of victim support reflect cultural differences between the countries concerned. However, attempts to standardise service provision (such as those by the Council of Europe, the EU and the United Nations) result from international agencies' recognition that victims have certain needs which go unmet in some countries because of the failure to give priority to service provision. Even in some wealthy and highly developed countries, services are rudimentary or non-existent. For example, in Spain, victims receive little legal recognition and no dedicated services. This is changing, but it took the Madrid train bombings and the dramatic fall of the previous government to bring about the conditions in which change could occur. Until that time, in the summer of 2004, little was being done to bring Spain into line with internationally agreed minimum standards for victim care.

This chapter has examined some of the problems arising from ill-conceived attempts to do things 'for' victims without appropriate consultation, although it has also covered the beneficial impact some of these innovations have also had. In Chapter Five, some less ambivalent success stories are considered.

Chapter Five

Real improvements for victims of crime

This chapter highlights examples of effective provision for victims of crime, using a series of case studies. In doing so, it pinpoints some of the lessons for good practice arising from these examples. A recurrent theme is the importance of hearing what victims themselves say about their needs: if services are to succeed in empowering victims, they need to start by listening to what victims have to say about their wishes, experiences and needs. Sometimes what victims say they want seems surprising or counter-intuitive, as some of these examples illustrate, but it is only if their wishes are sought in the first place that these will stand a chance of being articulated and met – particularly if what they say they want is not expected by the policymakers and practitioners concerned.

It is often possible to draw helpful lessons from negative feedback: many of the examples of services for victims given in the earlier chapters of this book have the potential to encourage improvements in future practice by facilitating learning from past mistakes. In the present chapter, however, the examples relate to successful and effective service provision which might usefully be emulated – suitably adapted for local circumstances – in other countries than those in which it currently exists.

This case study illustrates the benefits of responding to victims' expressed needs. It is unlikely that a service of this kind would have been provided had there been no evidence of need. In this particular case, victims contacted criminal justice agencies requesting contact with the offenders, and originally no mechanism for facilitating such meetings existed, still less any body of knowledge about how best to go about it. A careful process of assessment then

Case study: Victim–offender mediation in cases of serious violence

As discussed in Chapter Three, one of the criteria for effective restorative justice is the extent to which victims are involved in its implementation. The best restorative justice programmes pay close attention to victims' needs and facilitate their full involvement. In some cases, it is victims who request contact with 'their' offenders: the programmes which facilitate such contact in North America and in Europe have responded to this demand.

On the face of it, it may seem strange that a victim of a serious violent or sexual offence (or the family of a murder victim) should wish to make contact with the perpetrator. Until recently, criminal justice services generally saw no need to respond favourably to such requests, often resisting them because of the dangers and difficulties they foresaw, and victims had to work hard to set up contacts with offenders. This remains the case in many countries.

In Canada, and later in the USA and other jurisdictions, victims requested the opportunity to meet offenders for a variety of reasons. Considering the explanations such victims gave, it becomes apparent that they mirror the needs commonly expressed by victims generally: they wanted information; they wanted an opportunity to talk about what they had been through and express the psychological, social and material impact the crime had upon them and they hoped to achieve 'closure' or healthier grieving as a result. Additionally, in some cases, they hoped that the offender would be changed by the contact and dialogue with victims, and some victims and survivors had religious or spiritual motives connected with this aspiration (Umbreit *et al.* 1999; Buonatesta 2004). The initiative to date has almost invariably come from the victims in the North American projects, usually after an offender has been convicted (often years afterwards) (Umbreit 2001). The first Canadian project was preceded by research aimed at ascertaining the likely level of interest in using such a service (Gustafson and Smidstra 1989). This found that both the victims and the offenders in cases of severe violence were interested in meeting one another as long as the parties were properly prepared for the meetings and they took place in a safe and structured manner.

A pilot project was run in one correctional institution in 1991, and this was independently evaluated (Community Justice Initiatives 2004). It became clear that intensive preparation, sometimes over a lengthy period, was required, along with intensive, advanced training for the mediators (Umbreit 2001). The programme was expanded within Canada and, from the mid-1990s, similar programmes were set up by state Victim Services Units in the USA (Umbreit *et al.* 1999). A separate initiative was taken in Belgium in 2000, initially on an experimental basis, but the project was expanded and consolidated in subsequent years (Buonatesta 2004).

The eventual benefits for victims who took part in such carefully prepared meetings included feelings of relief, a reduction in fear and rage, and the feeling that the offender no longer exercised control over them. Some victims and survivors of murder victims had been consumed by hatred and were glad to let this go. Offenders reported emotional benefits too: they experienced feelings of empathy in some cases; some felt that they were more self-aware and less inwardly focused on the prison environment and some felt good about assisting victims. In the USA, victims sometimes withdrew their objections to the eventual release of the prisoner (although this is not an objective of such programmes and was not presented to the prisoners in advance as a likely outcome).

Victims sometimes found out things they would prefer not to have known, but they also felt relief at being able to reconstruct details of offences that had previously been unknown to them. One said:

> If forgiveness is defined as letting go of the anger and not letting the bitterness and anger and grief define me, then indeed I have forgiven them. I don't spend a lot of time thinking about it – or them. (Quoted in Umbreit 2001, p.272)

This illustrates what some victims mean when they speak of achieving closure. In a surprising number of cases, victims wished to 'help the good part' of the offender (Umbreit 2001, p.285). They hoped that by meeting him or her and expressing their emotions, they might draw out the offender's empathy towards victims and encourage him or her to avoid further violence in future. (Offender rehabilitation is a more explicit aim of the Belgian programme, on the basis that redress towards victims should in principle be an integral part of sentences of imprisonment, but also arising from a belief that it is inappropriate to contact victims only at the stage when the offender's release is being contemplated: see Collin and Guffens undated; Biermans 2002[1]).

Victims' family members were sometimes drawn to meet an offender because he or she was the last person to see the victim alive, and they had speculated (and in many cases had nightmares) about the manner of the victim's death. A meeting in such circumstances could help the survivors move on in their grieving process, and provide information which might help set their minds at rest. For many victims and survivors, the opportunity to hold the offender accountable in a face-to-face meeting was also important. They wanted to be able to show the offender how much emotional havoc they had caused, and how long-lasting its effects were.

Preparation of victims for such meetings has at times included letting them watch video recordings of previous mediation sessions, arranging a tour of the prison in which the offender was held before arranging a meeting with him or her and, in some cases, encouraging victims to lower their expectations of what might come out of a mediation session, in order to avoid any revictimisation that might result from disappointed hopes. Powerful emotions are clearly at work in these meetings, but it cannot be assumed that both parties will be honest or that they have no ulterior motives: this is where preparation and mediator training come into play. Follow-up meetings after a mediation session are also often required.

The Belgian programme is unique in being part of an attempt to change the culture of prisons. Restorative justice consultants in Belgian prisons are expected to 'act like ambassadors in our prisons, the messengers of the culture of restorative justice' (Biermans 2002, p.5). In addition to facilitating victim–offender mediation, they also attempt to improve the ways in which visiting victims are treated in prisons and to improve the services provided to prisoners who are victims. They have a general role in promoting a more respectful atmosphere within each prison, encouraging greater community involvement, including

---

1   According to Collin and Guffens (undated, p.1): 'It is important to underline the pluralist nature of the notion of reparation in this context. It concerns the victim and society equally, as well as the offender. It encompasses symbolic and material reparation of the damage caused to the victim, but also the restoration of the offender to his social position and the damage he, as the person responsible for the offence, has done to himself and his social circle.' In Belgium, victims can attend hearings of the meetings at which applications for conditional release are considered.

consultation with victims' organisations, and training staff in informal conflict resolution. They have come to recognise that prisoners may initially request contact with victims for selfish reasons to do with early release, yet it may nevertheless prove beneficial for the victim, and in some cases such contact should therefore be facilitated:

> it is not unusual for an initiative on the part of the offender, as an obvious spin-off of the conditional release process, to open up on the part of the victim a whole range of questions which unblock the possibility of a face-to-face meeting – a meeting which can be as intense as it was unexpected. (Buonatesta 2004, p.254[2])

This is not to suggest that such programmes should be offender-led: rather, they may open up new possibilities for dialogue in the interests of both parties. The prospect of the prisoner's release can raise powerful emotions on victims' part, and the opportunity to engage in such a dialogue can help them to deal with this. Mediation can reassure them about the offender's intentions and allow them to engage in discussion about the imposition of negotiated release conditions. Where such conditions are agreed between the parties, they seem more likely to be complied with than those imposed unilaterally (Buonatesta 2004).

These programmes are intensive and costly. The process is risky and could result in revictimisation if not managed sensitively. Several programmes have been evaluated, but the studies are relatively small-scale and the evaluators counsel caution about over-selling the programmes or relying too heavily on the findings from small samples of cases (see for example Umbreit *et al.* 1999). Nevertheless, they are an example of the criminal justice system responding positively to a demand made by victims, and they are unusual in the almost uniformly positive findings of evaluative research to date about their benefits for participants. Such experiments deserve to be carefully evaluated and, if found to be beneficial, emulated elsewhere.

---

2   Translated from French by the present author, as are the other quotations in this chapter.

began: potential participants' views were sought, and a possible need was established. A service was piloted in one institution, evaluated and then replicated. Appropriate practices and methods emerged in the process of experimentation. When the programme was seen to be successful on a small scale, it was adapted for use in other jurisdictions. In this sense, the victim–offender mediation programme in cases of severe violence could serve as a model for the development of new services for the victims of crime in any part of the world.

Case study: Involving female victims in work with male perpetrators of 'domestic' violence

When victims of violence within the home are asked what help they need, it is not unusual for them to respond that they want the partner to be helped to live non-violently: they want the assaults to stop (Morran, Andrew and Macrae 2002). Some of those who work with offenders have begun to take this seriously by involving the women in the work undertaken in response to the men's offending, taking care to do so in ways which protect the women's safety and confidentiality.

Two probation projects in Scotland have taken this approach, drawing upon the Duluth model of work with violent men developed in the USA in the late 1980s, and it has since been followed elsewhere (see Eadie and Knight 2002). Many of the traditional responses to male violence in the context of intimate relationships involve punishments which also have an adverse impact upon the offender's family (fines and short custodial sentences, for example; the family income is reduced by the punishment and the removal of the offender can create new problems for families in place of those it temporarily solves). Sentencers in Scottish cities asked for alternative disposals to these traditional sentences, and criminal justice social workers developed these in consultation with organisations working with victims. Violence against women and children within the home was understood by these workers in feminist terms, as intentional behaviour aimed at maintaining male dominance: the violence was functional for the men rather than resulting from a loss of control. Men were to be offered programmes, but not treated as if they were the victims, and the staff delivering such programmes generally took a pro-feminist stance (without necessarily using this terminology within the sponsoring agencies). Accordingly, the Change project was set up in Stirling in 1989 and the Domestic Violence Probation Project in Edinburgh the following year (Morran *et al.* 2002).

In an effort to avoid the disempowering effects of processing domestic violence solely within the criminal justice context, and in order to ensure the protection of the women complainants, these projects consult the women concerned as part of the process of assessing the offenders' suitability for probation with a condition of undertaking group work on their offending behaviour. The consultation process was designed in the light of advice from local Women's Aid groups, building upon their experience of working with victims, and involves both obtaining information about the offending behaviour and pattern and seeking the woman's assistance and co-operation in monitoring the man's behaviour while he remains under supervision. This process remains confidential: the man knows that his partner is to be approached, but that is all. If the woman chooses to tell him that she has not kept the appointments, her confidentiality will be respected. The women who stay with the abusive men are invited to complete a periodic behavioural checklist which alerts the project to warning signs: agreement to this process is a condition of the men's probation, although they remain unaware of what is said or even whether their partners take part in the process:

> In building this relationship with women [the project] is explicitly making the shift from seeing them as victims to treating them as consultants and experts on their partner's behaviour. (Morran *et al.* 2002, p.187)

By involving the women in this way, the project values their knowledge; but the women are also empowered by having the project's methodology explained to them in a way which enables them to make sense of men's controlling behaviour and the individual man's response to the programme: in this way, they can make informed decisions about their own safety. At the same time, a partner support worker provides a service to the women which is focused on their own, rather than their partners', needs (see Burton, Regan and Kelly 1998). The group work with the men aims to challenge their attitudes and encourage behavioural change, holding them accountable for the impact their offending has had upon their partners and any children involved. Evaluative research has shown the work to be generally effective (but see Eadie and Knight 2002). However, it is all but impossible to demonstrate a causal link between men's involvement in the programme and their subsequent behaviour, particularly in relation to offences of violence within the home, where recorded offending rates are notoriously unreliable. The programmes clearly only work for some men: others attempt to use their involvement to manipulate partners' feelings and get back together with them: 'one of the dangers of running a perpetrator programme is the implicit message that it gives to women that their partner might change. This can give women false hope' (McCarthy 2004, p.4).

Nevertheless, the cumulative evidence of thousands of behavioural checklists has made it possible to measure attitudinal as well as behavioural changes, and domestic violence arises from a desire to maintain control over a partner – an attitude which is susceptible to measurement and change (see Dobash *et al.* 2000; Wilson, M. 2003; www.changeweb.org.uk).

This case study demonstrates that services for offenders as well as those specifically designed for victims can be delivered in victim-centred ways. Protection, and even empowerment, can be delivered to victims as part of the supervision of offenders, given sufficient thought, commitment and the necessary resources. In this case, the process began with dissatisfaction with the outcomes of existing provision, and the change process involved consultation with victims' organisations as well as making use of research on victims' views. This resulted in innovative ways of involving, protecting and consulting victims, combined with an imaginative process for facilitating change in offenders' attitudes and behaviour. Although the projects have not always been well resourced, the knowledge they have gathered will not be lost because of the commitment of project staff to recording their successes and having their work independently evaluated. The workers involved have also set up a network called Respect, which promotes best practice and also runs an advice line for perpetrators seeking help to stop assaulting their partners (www.respect.uk.net). The Scottish projects have been replicated by probation areas in England and Wales, and there are at least 30 group-work programmes for offenders (mostly accepting self-referrals from perpetrators wishing to take part). In addition, the National Probation Service in England and Wales has had two programmes accredited for use nationally, although they do not follow the Change project model in all respects (McCarthy 2004).

The knowledge gained by these projects has also been transferred to probation work with high-risk offenders, at least in some parts of the country. For example, a specialist version of Multi-Agency Public Protection Panels (MAPPPs) has been established in Cardiff to ensure that a dedicated service is provided to victims in severe cases of domestic violence. When Multi-Agency

Risk Assessment Conferences (MARACs) are held in these cases, women's self-help organisations are represented, and the risk presented by the offender is assessed using criteria informed by experience of working with serious violent offenders in such cases.[3] Inter-agency working has improved understanding of work with victims of this kind of crime, and of the risks involved. A specialist, 'fast-track domestic violence court' was established in 2002 with the aim of increasing women's safety and keeping them fully informed about cases (an initiative which is not unique to Cardiff). An independent evaluation of MARAC revealed the importance of taking women's intuition about potential escalation of violence seriously, and procedures have been amended accordingly. It also demonstrated that revictimisation had been reduced significantly for the project's clients (Robinson 2004).

As with the previous case study (of victim–offender mediation in cases of serious violence), the wishes of victims that the system should concentrate upon helping offenders to change rather than punishing them might seem surprising. By taking this insight into victims' needs seriously, a service has been devised which appears to meet that objective in an impressive proportion of the cases it deals with.

Case study: Witness support

The idea for a Witness Service in England and Wales arose from the work of a committee set up by Victim Support to consider the needs of witnesses at court, followed by a piece of action research also commissioned by Victim Support (NAVSS 1988; Raine and Smith 1991). The committee's report identified problems for victims both before court and at court, and recommended improved training for ushers, magistrates, judges, lawyers and police officers as well as calling for Victim Support to place volunteers in the busier courts to assist witnesses. Clearer and more information was required by witnesses in advance and on the day; witnesses should be given more notice of court dates and warned of likely delays in cases being heard; and the accessibility, comfort and safety of waiting areas required attention (NAVSS 1988). The action research project involved a pilot project in seven English Crown Courts

---

3   Risk factors include jealous or controlling behaviour by the perpetrator, previous police call-outs for domestic violence, relationship separation, escalating seriousness and frequency of abuse, perpetrators with aggravating problems (Robinson 2004).

from 1989. The research found that victims were often apprehensive and ill-informed about court procedures, and many experienced distressing meetings with offenders and those accompanying them to court. Most felt there was insufficient consultation when court dates were fixed, and many would have welcomed more information being provided both before and at court. Eighty-six per cent of respondents thought it was important to have waiting areas for witnesses separate from the place where defendants waited. The researchers recommended the establishment of a Witness Service at all Crown Courts as soon as possible, using a combination of paid staff and volunteers and reaching out to provide a similar service to magistrates' courts (Raine and Smith 1991).

The Witness Service was extended to a number of other Crown Courts in England and Wales in 1994, achieving national coverage two years later. The Home Office commissioned further research in 1996, and the final report, published the following year, identified a range of problems faced by witnesses and recommended improvements in the treatment of vulnerable witnesses as well as the provision of a specific service to defence and prosecution witnesses in all magistrates' courts (Plotnikoff and Woolfson 1997). Many of these changes were introduced in the 1999 Youth Justice and Criminal Evidence Act, discussed in Chapter One. The Witness Service was then introduced in magistrates' courts from 1999 to 2002, and in Scottish Sheriff Courts from 1996. It is currently being extended to cover the High Court in Scotland, and in practice Witness Services are also routinely being allowed access to youth courts in England and Wales to provide an equivalent service to those witnesses involved in cases where the offender happens to be a young person (Victim Support undated).

Being a witness is a stressful experience; people's expectations cause concern even when the actual experience does not bear them out. Those who have experience of courts may have seen aggressive questioning of witnesses in previous cases; those who have no direct experience may well have seen dramatised versions of cross-examination on TV. Some witnesses are called at short notice, and many have to miss work or report to court after working a night shift. Giving evidence worries people partly because they do not know what to expect, and it is always worrying when one feels one has no control over one's environment (Jenkins 2002). Typically, prospective witnesses' fears include being asked questions they are unable to answer, not understanding what is happening in court, having to wait a long time to give their evidence and not knowing what impact the experience of cross-examination might have upon them (Raine and

Smith 1991; Plotnikoff and Woolfson 1998). None of this is really surprising, given the arcane language and procedures used, particularly in the higher courts. Victims in particular have reason to expect the experience to be disheartening. Sometimes, witnesses are repeatedly summonsed to attend court, only to be sent away when cases are adjourned. Offenders may do deals with the prosecution and obtain more lenient sentences by plea-bargaining, they may be sentenced in ways that victims regard as insufficiently punitive or they may not be convicted at all. Very often, these processes occur without any consultation with victims (Williams 2000). The defence may cast aspersions on victims in the course of eliciting evidence and victims have no effective right of reply (derogatory statements to be made in pleas of mitigation should, in theory, be disclosed to the prosecution in advance, but this rarely happens in practice and there is little incentive for prosecutors to challenge them) (Home Office 1999). These factors can add to the stress involved in giving evidence.

The Witness Service exists to support both prosecution and defence witnesses, and this is important in terms of its impartiality, although in practice it works almost entirely with prosecution witnesses. It provides a range of services which are designed to put witnesses at ease and reassure them about giving evidence. Before the case comes to court, some witnesses find it helpful to visit the court building and, if possible, a court-room. This can help to prepare them for what is involved in giving evidence, not least in terms of familiarising themselves with the layout of the court. Such visits are arranged by Witness Service staff. Arrangements can also be made for witnesses to enter the building by another door than the public entrance if necessary. Witnesses are sent standardised information about court procedures by the Witness Service (and they should also be told about the government's 'virtual walk-through' website, which provides a good deal of illustrated information – and some degree of reassurance – about the experience of giving evidence: see www.cjsonline.gov.uk/witness/walkthrough/). In newer court buildings, the Witness Service has its own office with a place for witnesses to wait, apart from the communal waiting rooms where offenders and their families are waiting. This can be important for witnesses who are nervous about running into the offender unexpectedly, and for those who have been threatened. Where necessary, the police witness protection or victim liaison staff will liaise with the Witness Service to ensure that witnesses' distress is minimised.

The wait to go into court can be a long one, and refreshments are available. During the case itself, volunteers are available to accompany witnesses in court. They are trained in court procedures and they are aware that they must not discuss the evidence (for fear of 'contaminating' the witnesses' testimony), give legal advice or make conversation. Their presence is purely symbolic and supportive, but this is reassuring for some people and, of course, they explain in advance why they are forbidden to interact with witnesses while in the court-room. In practice, not many witnesses make use of this aspect of the service: Scottish research found that it occurred in only 0.5 per cent of cases (Lobley and Smith 2003). The safeguards on Witness Service interactions with witnesses will remain necessary as long as the courts continue to regard the principle that evidence should be subject to cross-examination as something close to sacrosanct. The continuing centrality of the legal doctrine that seeing and hearing witnesses give their evidence, and then questioning them about it, is the best way to test the evidence (the principle of orality) makes other, more radical changes to the experience of giving evidence in criminal trials unlikely in the foreseeable future (Ellison 2001).

After their court appearance, witnesses often need to express their feelings about how they were treated. They may bitterly regret their involvement with the criminal justice system, and after cross-examination many witnesses feel that their word has been doubted by the court (Williams 2002). The Witness Service can provide an opportunity for them to ventilate their feelings and provide a pretext for doing so by offering to help them fill in their expenses claim forms. Witnesses will also be put in touch with whoever can answer any specific questions they may have about the case (Spackman 2000). The Witness Service has regular meetings with other court users, which provide an opportunity to take up issues about the treatment of witnesses and the facilities available for them with the appropriate bodies.

This service responds to the concerns expressed by victims and other witnesses, and to the research evidence about the pressures involved in giving evidence in court (Murray 1997; Temkin 1997, 2002). It takes account of the legal constraints involved in supporting witnesses without appearing to 'coach' them about their testimony, and it provides unobtrusive support to the great majority of victims and witnesses attending court, which for many of them is a difficult time. Like its parent organisation, Victim Support, it demonstrates community concern for people under stress as a result of crime by providing neighbourly support. Many witnesses have only brief contact with the service but some require more intensive support, and most are grateful for its existence (Lobley and Smith 2003).

This case study illustrates the process by which a need identified both by academic research and by Victim Support, in response to concerns raised by individual victims, was met. Substantial resources have been made available by central government in recognition of the value of the service, which was originally piloted and then made available in the higher courts before being replicated in a slightly different form in magistrates' courts, then in Scotland. Government commitment to the Witness Service may well be motivated primarily by a concern to improve witnesses' attendance rates at court and by a reluctance to challenge the dominance of the principle of orality, but the practical effect has been to provide help to large numbers of witnesses who might otherwise have received none. Concerns about possible interference with the legal process were met by separating the new service administratively and practically from local Victim Support schemes in the community, and introducing distinct training programmes for the volunteers which emphasise the importance of legal processes and the rights of the parties. The service is provided by an agency with considerable experience of determining and meeting victims' needs, and it has responded to what is known about the needs of both defence and prosecution witnesses.

Victim empowerment through victim-centred policy

In some of the cases discussed above change has arisen, not primarily from a concern to improve victims' experiences of the criminal justice system, but because the system needs a better response from victims for its own purposes. For example, the motivation for improving the experiences of witnesses at courts, including those defined as vulnerable, was primarily to reduce the number of 'cracked' trials[4] and to enable witnesses to give the best evidence they could (thus increasing the likelihood of defendants being convicted). A secondary motivation was to meet government targets in relation to improving public confidence in the criminal justice system. Nevertheless, survey evidence shows that vulnerable and intimidated witnesses' levels of satisfaction with how they were treated at court have improved, and they are (overall) less fearful about – and less distressed by – important aspects of the experi-

---

4   'Cracked' trials are those in which the defendant pleads guilty at the last moment; this wastes public money and the time of prosecution witnesses. Some defendants are advised to deny guilt in the hope that witnesses may not turn up at court or may be intimidated – but legal scholars question how frequently this really occurs (McConville 2002).

ence than they were until recently (Hamlyn *et al.* 2004). It seems highly likely that this is directly related to the provision of special measures under the 1999 Youth Justice and Criminal Evidence Act, and the work of the Witness Service. Whatever the government's motives for introducing these changes, they have improved the experience of witnesses attending court and reduced the stress experienced by significant numbers of victims. Victim empowerment may not directly result from such measures, but these are significant achievements in themselves, and in some circumstances they may represent a step towards greater empowerment.[5]

Similarly, restorative justice initiatives often have at their roots a desire to help the offenders (to change, to take charge of their lives) and, as discussed in Chapter Three, this may lead to a marginalisation or neglect of victims' needs in what is meant to be a balanced victim- and offender-focused approach. The case study in the present chapter shows that restorative justice can, if it is designed with victims' needs at the forefront, help them to move on and take charge of their lives. Victims in cases of severe violence in a number of countries expressed a need to confront, question and challenge the perpetrators, and when they did so in carefully controlled circumstances they found that this met their emotional needs. In some cases they attended a single meeting which met these needs; in others, they got to know the offender in mediated discussions over a period of time. In both cases, the experience usually helped them to achieve some degree of peace of mind. For some it went further, and they were able to engage in constructive discussion with the authorities and sometimes with the offenders themselves, about the circumstances in which they could contemplate conditional release of the prisoner (which in many countries would occur whether or not victims were involved in the decision-making process). This, too, can be seen as an empowering process.

Work with perpetrators of 'domestic' violence aimed at changing their attitudes and behaviour has begun to grapple with questions about how best to protect and involve the partners concerned. This is empowering in an important sense, particularly when combined with the provision of other services which help to clarify and open up the choices available to the women

---

5   Everything depends, however, upon the ways in such measures are implemented. There have been cases of special measures being granted on application by the prosecution service, which cannot subsequently be reversed if a witness objects to being 'protected' from giving live evidence. This kind of paternalistic approach is hardly empowering for witnesses who feel strong enough to give evidence and wish to do so.

concerned. Not only are the offenders held directly (and as far as the women are concerned, confidentially) accountable: they are also forced to accept that other stakeholders have a legitimate interest in their violent behaviour and that their victims are among this number. While the project described remains essentially experimental, it offers an interesting model of victim involvement in the design of solutions to offenders' problems which also impinge upon the victims' freedom to live their lives as they choose. It has also been influential in the establishment of services in other parts of the UK.

The final case study, of the introduction of services for witnesses in the courts, is a more traditional example of responding to identified needs and providing new services for victims. It is important in the context of victim empowerment because it found ways of overcoming objections of principle on the part of other powerful actors within the criminal justice system and because it began by identifying the specific frustrations and concerns of witnesses before contemplating the provision of a service. In a very simple way, it provided a means for witnesses to participate more comfortable and more fully in the criminal justice process.

It is apparent from these case studies that it is possible to involve victims and victim advocacy groups in the design and provision of criminal justice services, and that even services specifically for offenders can benefit from this input. At best, victim empowerment can result. At worst, services at least become more sensitive to the needs of victims of crime. While it is increasingly common for victim support agencies to be consulted as part of the process of drafting and introducing new legislation, it remains comparatively unusual for them to be involved in the detailed design of projects. The case studies show that this is possible and practicable, and that it can have positive results – not only for victims. The examples given may not necessarily be readily transferable from one legal system to another, but the principles which emerge from the case studies have general validity: it is worthwhile to involve and consult victims and the organisations which have experience in working with them; it is likely that service design and delivery will be improved by hearing what they have to say and the public legitimacy of the system can only be improved in the process. Some of the examples given in this chapter relate to programmes which have in fact been successfully piloted in one country and then adapted for use elsewhere: although it is always wise to be cautious about the possible unintended effects of policy transfer (Zedner 1995), it is equally the case that good ideas tend to travel quickly.

Chapter Six

Conclusions

Changing approaches to meeting victims' needs within criminal justice

Understanding of the needs and aspirations of victims of crime has increased enormously over the past forty years, although the pace of change has varied from one country to another and from time to time depending on political changes. Those attempting to speak for victims have become much more sophisticated in their arguments and in their engagement with the political process during this period, and the responses have in turn become gradually more appropriate and more carefully calibrated to meet established needs. Research into victims' wishes and needs and into the success or otherwise of policy initiatives has increasingly informed decision-making. However, criminal justice policy is often characterised by a preoccupation with short-term outcomes and – all too often – with gimmickry. It is a commonplace observation to note that victims of crime have become a political football (Elias 1993; Williams 1999a; Walklate 2004). It is, as Walklate notes, disrespectful to victims to use them in this way – and victims feel this acutely themselves. At times, the attempts to enlist victims in aid of a particular political campaign have proved relatively harmless – perhaps even incidentally benign – despite the virtual irrelevance of the changes concerned to victims' real needs. This was arguably the case in relation to the first draft of the UK Victim's Charter, from which some good eventually came despite its promulgation without consultation with most of the agencies affected by its provisions, the irrelevance of some of the changes it introduced and its overtly political motivation (see Chapter One and Williams 1999a, 1999b; Zaubermann 2000). However, other changes have been made primarily for political reasons, ignoring the evidence of their likely impact upon victims, and these have sometimes inadvertently harmed both victims' interests and their confidence in the criminal justice system: an example, discussed in Chapters One and Four, is the introduction of the Victim Personal Statement scheme in England and Wales. While such statements may be beneficial for some victims in some circumstances, this knowledge was not harnessed effectively in implementing what was arguably a presentational change made for political effect.

Some of the trends described earlier in this book have profoundly affected victims of crime despite their peripheral involvement in these developments. The movements towards community justice and restorative justice are good examples. Although ensuring a better experience for victims of crime may have been one of the aims of those arguing for such changes, this has rarely been their central motivation and, as a result, services for victims have often been introduced from an offender-led perspective and as an after-thought. An example of this, discussed in Chapters One and Four, is the introduction of statutory compensation for victims of violent and sexual offences; the likely impact of this compensation on victims was completely unknown at the time when it was launched. It has been suggested that its implementation arose partly from a political need to 'do something for victims' because many people at the time believed that too much was being done for offenders (Rock 1990). This does not necessarily mean that criminal justice reform which is motivated by a desire to improve matters for offenders and their communities, or by a paternalistic but ill-informed desire to help victims themselves, will inevitably serve victims badly: far from it. There can be both incidental and planned benefits for victims from such changes, as discussed in Chapters Two, Three and Four. Such a history is far from ideal, though, and it has often led to distortions in victim services designed with more than half an eye on offenders' interests.

In the case of the move towards community justice, this is a significant issue. Advocates of community justice blithely argue that it involves new responsibilities as well as new rights both for offenders and for victims. As discussed in Chapter Two, victims are characterised by some community justice enthusiasts as part of a network of mutual obligations (for example, see Clear and Karp 2000), when they have not been consulted about this reorientation of the system and its likely benefits for them are by no means clear. However, this may merely be the result of unduly ebullient rhetoric on the part of community justice advocates: it is clear from the discussion in Chapter Two that greater accountability on the part of offenders is potentially in victims' interests, as in the cases of circles of support and accountability and of community justice centres. Both initiatives strengthen the case for community justice as potentially beneficial to victims. More flexibility on the part of official criminal justice agencies was also clearly seen to be of potential benefit to victims, as in the *No Witness, No Justice* pilot projects and the resultant changes to the treatment of witnesses in England and Wales also discussed in Chapter Two.

Victims and the organisations supporting them do not object to the stated principles of community justice: it is likely to be in everyone's interests to have more responsive, informal, accessible, local and personalised justice characterised by greater stakeholder participation. The important question is how these aspirations are put into effect, and how central victims' needs and wishes are to their implementation. Christie's (1977) vision of the 'victim-oriented court' is very attractive and its realisation depends heavily upon principles such as flexibility, accessibility, informality and lay decision-making.

If community justice initiatives can be shown conclusively to reduce re-offending, this will be good for victims in the long term – but this has yet to be established, until rigorous evaluations of the various initiatives described in Chapter Two, and others like them, are completed. Levels of victim involvement in many ostensibly victim-centred community justice projects have been disturbingly low, and we need to know why this is the case and how it might be addressed. The complacent response of some evaluators to this issue is unsatisfactory: Karp (2004, p.61), for example, notes with apparent regret the low levels of participation by victims in the Vermont boards, but goes on to blame 'the logistical challenges of implementation and, ultimately, the disinterest [sic] of victims'. Why were victims not interested? How might their levels of interest be increased? Is it actually in their interests to become more involved? If, like so many community justice initiatives, the boards were mainly driven by a desire to divert offenders from costly prisons and rehabilitate them more effectively, why should victims want to take part in their work, unless there are clear benefits for them?

Part of the answer may lie with the principles of restorative justice, scrutinised in respect of a number of examples from different parts of the world in Chapter Three. Like community justice, restorative justice has not been as rigorously evaluated as one might wish – and all too often the evaluation which has taken place has neglected victim perspectives. Another thing restorative justice has in common with community justice is the tendency of its proponents to argue that it is beneficial for victims, but to design restorative programmes with greater attention to offender-led objectives than to concern for victims. This often leads to skewed projects which give undue priority to offender interests, despite the fundamental principle that restorative justice is supposed to balance the interests of victims, offenders and the community. Using victims in the service of objectives such as punishment, rehabilitation or other types of change to offenders' attitudes and behaviour may be justifiable in some circumstances, but in practice it tends to push victims' own concerns to the margins. All too often, poor practice in relation to ascertaining and meeting victims' wishes, rights and needs has prevented them from obtaining the potential benefits of involvement in restorative interventions (Maxwell and Morris 2001).

However, restorative justice does have such potential benefits for victims. If properly planned and resourced, it can lead to lowered levels of anger and fear on the part of victims, especially in cases where agreement has been reached between offenders and victims (and in those cases, particularly when the commitments made are honoured by the offender). It has generally beneficial effects which are as helpful to victims as they are to other parties, such as greater informality, quicker resolution of disputes, an enhanced sense of fairness and reduced rates of re-offending (although further evidence in the latter respect is required: see McIvor 2004). Victims involved in restorative justice are generally better informed about the progress of their cases than those involved with the conventional criminal justice system, although substantial improvements are still needed in the provision of information to victims. Restorative justice is far more likely, also, to result in compensation, reparation or an apology being made to the victim. It is also well established that restorative interventions can make it more probable that victims achieve a sense of closure, especially in more serious cases. It seems that in many cases, too, the preparation process involved in setting up restorative meetings can be therapeutically helpful for victims (although here, again, there is a lack of robust research evidence). Where victims and offenders meet, there is undoubtedly often a benefit for victims in terms of reassurance that the offender is not as formidable or frightening in person as the victim had anticipated, and in many cases offenders undertake in front of witnesses whose opinion matters to them not to repeat the offence against the individual concerned.

Overall, this is an impressive list of potential benefits. Victims' organisations have begun to be persuaded that it is worthwhile to become involved in restorative justice, both for individual victims and for the victim support agencies themselves, which can have an important role in project design and implementation. Restorative justice is no panacea, but it has considerable potential to improve the position of victims within criminal justice, if victims' needs and wishes are properly taken into account in the design and delivery of projects.

A more balanced approach to defining and serving the victim: Meeting victims' needs without attacking offenders' rights

It is clear that the 'zero sum game' approach to victims' rights is ill-conceived and potentially dangerous. As demonstrated in Chapter Four, there is no need to attack the rights and services allocated to offenders in order to improve matters for victims. Indeed, victim policy should not normally be devised by looking at provision for offenders at all: while the two are related, victim-centred policies are unlikely to derive from an approach which starts by thinking about offenders. Provision for offenders should be improved for its own sake and if that process leads to incidental benefits for victims such as a reduction in re-offending that is all well and good. Simultaneously, there are good reasons for improving services to victims. Reducing offenders' rights and removing offender services in order to redistribute resources is cynical, illogical and ultimately unhelpful to victims' interests.

One of the potential benefits of restorative justice is eliciting forgiveness towards offenders by victims, ensuring peaceful future relations. The difference of opinion between the judge, Lord Bingham, and the Lord Chief Justice of England and Wales discussed in Chapter Four is a revealing one in this respect. While the latter, in a policy document written at an abstract level, regarded victims' views on sentencing as irrelevant (and by implication, as an unhelpful distraction from sentencers' task), Lord Bingham felt compelled to hear and respond to the victims' views when confronted with them in an actual case. Two victims wanted him to know why they did not wish to see an offender imprisoned and why it would be better for them if he were not. In some ways, this is analogous to the different ways in which policy on victims can be made. Politicians have a choice between (at one extreme) exploiting 'the victim' for ideological reasons and (ideally) hearing what real victims have to say and acting on this information. While a number of the innovations discussed in Chapter Four were quite successfully improving victim services, what many of them had in common was that they were imposed without thorough consultation. Statutory compensation was introduced partly as a sop to those who felt that too much was being done for offenders and that victims ought to take a turn in the limelight (Rock 1990). Whether it was actually what victims needed was, in that context, beside the point. While victims have gained a great deal of benefit from the compensation scheme, it has been costly and it is questionable whether it was the best use of public funds for helping victims.

Similarly, Victim Personal Statements were a cheap way of appearing to offer a more central role to 'the victim', and they were imported from the USA with some modifications to reflect the difficulties experienced in introducing them there – but without taking proper account of the findings of research on the pilot projects, which found them to be of very limited benefit to victims as delivered during the experimental period. Subsequent experience has borne out the predictions of the research team: few statements seem to make it out of the police stations in which they are taken and, even when they do, their value to sentencers and victims is limited. A combination of scepticism on the part of victims themselves and resistance to change by criminal justice practitioners (in this case, probably at least partly justified) has rendered the initiative largely ineffective.

A more successful experience has been the introduction of an information exchange mechanism with victims by the probation service. However, its launch was botched, unsurprisingly given the lack of consultation or any new resources for its establishment. It took several years for the probation service to make sense of the policy with which it was presented in the Victim's Charter, and in most areas it was nearly a decade before the victim contact service was properly established. It is a tribute to the professionalism of the probation service that, by the late 1990s, victims in more serious cases were systematically being offered a choice about the information they received on the progress of their cases and the offenders involved, and the service was ensuring that the information wanted was routinely provided. Given the centrality of information provision among the needs identified by victims of crime, this is an important advance. It is unfortunate that it was introduced in such a piecemeal, half-hearted way, but subsequent research has shown how beneficial such a service can be to victims.

Some success stories in relation to services for victims are more wholehearted than these examples, and Chapter Five relates a number of these. They have a number of factors in common: experience of an identified need led to research which in turn guided the design of pilot projects. Sometimes legislation was the result, but in other cases new, victim-focused practices were introduced on the basis of what had been learnt, without the need for changes in the law. Services continued (and continue) to develop in the light of what was learnt from experience. The lessons of practice in one country could then in some cases be cautiously applied to the development of similar services elsewhere. Thus, the introduction of victim–offender mediation in cases of serious violence in Canada was carefully researched and piloted, allowing some initial lessons to be learnt before attempting similar approaches in the USA, Belgium and elsewhere. Similarly, group work with perpetrators of domestic violence in the UK drew upon US experience and research, and it was piloted in Scotland before being adapted for wider use in England and Wales. In this case, the friendly but critical reactions and suggestions of colleagues in external organisations such as Women's Aid enabled statutory services to monitor and improve their practice with offenders in the interests of the victims.

The gradual, phased introduction of the Witness Service in England and Wales was preceded both by research into witnesses' needs and by an action research project which piloted and adapted the recommended model of witness support. The outcome was not only the introduction of a new service; the research also informed the consultation process which eventually resulted in legislation on the protection of vulnerable witnesses. Like its predecessor the Victim Support scheme, the local Witness Service has become a model for similar arrangements in a number of other countries in the British Isles and much further afield.

A more balanced approach to defining and serving the victim: Widening the scope of law and policy

Services for victims of crime tend to be provided mainly to the victims of conventionally defined crimes, such as offences against property or the person, committed by individuals. This means that the victims of other types of crime are often neglected. For example, the victimisation suffered by people subject to organised crimes such as trafficking in people and the consequences of corporate crime for individuals are often not recognised by the current, individualised model of victim support (which in turn reflects a criminal justice system focused upon individual events and perpetrators). The implications for policy and service provision are considered in this section.

New types of crime throw up new categories of victims, but the process of claiming or attributing victim status is a complex one. An obvious example is domestic violence, which was largely invisible to policymakers until the mid-1970s (see Mawby and Walklate 1994, Chapter 4). Only when feminist campaigns and service provision in the form of women's refuges made it impossible to ignore, did official thinking begin to catch up with social reality. The balance of power gradually shifted, reflecting wider social changes. There is a notion of the 'ideal victim' which has to be challenged in order to allow new groups of victims to be recognised. The 'ideal victim' is created by stereotyping, both within the news media and more generally. While this is by no means a new phenomenon (see Christie 1986; Hartless *et al.* 1995), it is a persistent one. The image conjured up by the phrase 'victim of crime' remains, for many people, that of someone like an elderly woman having her handbag snatched in the street. Such a victim fits the stereotype in all respects: she is perceived as vulnerable, innocent, unable to fight back and therefore deserving sympathy and help. The social and political consensus has changed to allow women who report assaults by their partners to be accommodated within the ideal type, but only when they are perceived as blameless victims. Once they depart from this stereotype, they are likely to be blamed for their victimisation or questioned about whether it really occurred, in much the same way as those reporting domestic violence found themselves treated before the problem was generally recognised.

The issue of the 'ideal victim' also has a bearing upon access to and take-up of services. For example, a young woman who has been abducted from her home in eastern Europe and forced to work as a prostitute in the UK is likely to be treated by official agencies first as an illegal immigrant and only second, if at all, as a victim of crime. She is far from the stereotypical victim of crime: she has no right to be in the country in the first place and she works in the sex trade, albeit under duress. She is, nevertheless, in need of protection and access to services – both of which are in very short supply for people in these sorts of circumstances in the UK. Power and the lack of power are important determining factors here. The following case study relates to a real, but disguised, case.

As already noted, Alenka is far from being an 'ideal' victim. One view of her situation is that she is a child in need of protection and a traumatised victim of the serious offences of repeated rapes, kidnapping and living off immoral earnings. An alternative interpretation is that she is an economic migrant and an illegal immigrant. The latter view is the one taken in most parts of the UK, and people like Alenka are deported without much attention being paid to the unlawful activities of their pimps and traffickers or to their own needs and suffering. Because of the dominant view of prostitution and the confusion about the law, victims are criminalised and their 'customers' (most of whom must know that they are visiting trafficked women) are not. As Siân Jones of Amnesty International points out, few men visiting eastern European prostitutes can be unaware of the coercion used by their pimps: 'Here, there is absolutely no meaningful consent at all. It is clear that if you

---

Case study: Trafficking in people

A 15-year-old girl, Alenka, was kidnapped in Timisaora, Romania, and taken to Albania, where she was raped at gunpoint by her abductor. She subsequently met a woman called Vera, who told her that her daughter worked in England and would help her find a job there. Vera's friend Tomas took Alenka by boat to Italy, and then overland to Belgium. Vera's husband Stanislav met them from the ferry and took Alenka to London. He then told her that her journey had cost him a great deal of money and that she owed him £3000. She was required to work in his 'sauna' to repay the debt. She had to have sex with large numbers of men every night. All her earnings were given to Stanislav, who threatened her with a knife on one occasion when he found a telephone number in her purse. She eventually escaped and was put in contact with the Metropolitan Police Vice Squad. When she found out that she would probably be deported as an illegal immigrant she fled the country, and she is unwilling to give evidence against anyone involved in the offences against her. Stanislav has been successfully prosecuted for an unrelated offence of burglary but the police have been unable to charge him with any offence against Alenka (based on the account in Gibb 2003).

---

knowingly have sex with a woman who has been trafficked, that is rape' (quoted in Vulliamy 2004, p.29).

This is not, however, the view taken by the police and the immigration authorities in the UK in such cases. Men using prostitutes are not criminalised, although in other circumstances rape carries a sentence of life imprisonment, and protection for young trafficked women is only available to a small number of them at one shelter in London, run by the Poppy Project. This is funded by the Home Office, and its help is provided only on condition that trafficked women agree to provide information about the perpetrators to the police. However, Britain also signed a bilateral agreement with the Albanian government in 2003 to repatriate trafficked women, some of whom have since been sent home only to be trafficked again (Vulliamy 2004). Official policy seems contradictory.

Other approaches are possible. In Sweden, the buying of sexual services was made illegal in 1999, since when the number of prostitutes in major cities such as Stockholm has substantially reduced. The Council of Europe is drafting a convention on trafficking which will require member states to provide protection and support to trafficked people, building upon previous measures against the traffickers themselves (partly in response to criticism from voluntary agencies working with trafficked women, such as Amnesty International and Anti-Slavery International, whose comments on early drafts of the new convention pointed out that there had thus far been considerably more attention paid to traffickers than to their victims).

Non-governmental organisations working in the field have argued for three basic standards to be met by the convention. First, they say that governments should provide support, shelter and safety for women who manage to escape from traffickers. This requires additional training for those who will come into contact with trafficked women, including the police. Second, the women should be given time to think about whether it is in their interests to co-operate with police investigations into the activities of the traffickers (often, victims' families in their home countries are threatened, and some relatives have been killed when trafficked women in the UK went to the police, so this needs serious consideration). Third, residence permits should be provided, particularly when women are at risk, either of violence or of being trafficked again, if they return to their home countries. The Italian government already has such a system, which no doubt helps to explain why women are trafficked across Italy to destinations such as the UK (Vulliamy 2004). Immigration is a sensitive issue in Italy, as in the UK, but the need to prevent trafficking and protect its potential victims was given priority there. Even before the introduction of a specific law on trafficking in 2003, which provides for a maximum penalty of 20 years' imprisonment, the existing law was used to mount a substantial number of effective prosecutions. This includes the use of a provision of immigration law which allows a 'stay permit for social protection' so that victims need not fear deportation: these are being issued at the rate of several hundred per year. Alongside this, non-governmental organisations offer victims effective support (Curtol *et al.* 2004), although the police do not appear to have good witness protection arrangements or to regard trafficked women primarily as victims of crime (Goodey 2004).

Trafficking in people is extremely lucrative for the criminals involved and less risky than trading in illegal drugs (Egan and Millar 2004). The United Nations estimated in 2003 that it resulted in seven billion dollars of profit annually (Erez, Ibarra and McDonald 2004). Once someone has accepted the offer made by a people trafficker, they cease to be regarded as a person: they come to be seen as a commodity. Victims of trafficking are potentially profitable 'goods', and they are 'easier to transport, use and re-use than [in] the trafficking of illegal drugs or arms' (Egan and Millar 2004, p.9). Only by reducing the demand, as in Sweden, and increasing the level of risk of prosecution, as in Italy, will traffickers be persuaded that the risks of this type of crime are becoming too high. Alongside this, there is a need for greater understanding of the real role of the women involved in such crimes: they are not accomplices but victims of organised crime. This understanding has been increased by the work of the United Nations, the Council of Europe and the Organisation for Security and Co-operation in Europe,[1] although many of the policy responses by member states have been limited and the practical measures put in place are often short term (Goodey 2005), as in the case of UK funding of the Poppy Project. In 2000, the United Nations adopted a Protocol on trafficking,[2] aimed at demand reduction, increased border security, the promotion of employment opportunities in the women's countries of origin and the provision of information campaigns making them aware of the dangers involved in accepting employment abroad. In countries where the law enforcement agencies are not corrupt, this may help – but attitudes have to change, both in the receiving countries and the countries of origin, before the problem can be effectively tackled.

Although much serious crime is now carried out by apparently respectable business people, often across national borders, crime and its victims are not routinely conceptualised in these ways. Consequently, policy responses to globalised crime prove inadequate, both in terms of apprehending offenders and in the ways they respond to victims. The preoccupation with the right to cross-examine witnesses face to face in court in countries such as the UK (the 'principle of orality') means that witness protection becomes a major issue (Egan and Millar 2004), whereas in other jurisdictions, trafficking and other organised crime is disrupted effectively by seizing offenders' assets, which need not involve victims at all (Goodey 2004), an approach which has recently been adopted in the UK for the first time (see Footnote 2). However,

---

1   The OSCE has encouraged and disseminated victim-sensitive approaches to trafficking; see www.osce.org/news/show_news.php?id=4385. These are intended to be reflected in domestic laws enacted in individual countries. The United Nations has agreed a Protocol to Prevent, Suppress and Punish Trafficking in Persons, especially Women and Children and this was followed by an EU framework decision on Trafficking for Sexual and Labour Exploitation in 2002. In the UK, this led directly to the creation of new imprisonable offences of trafficking in the Nationality, Immigration and Asylum Act 2002 and the Sexual Offences Act 2003. In addition, traffickers' assets may now be seized under the Proceeds of Crime Act 2002.

2   The UN Protocol to Prevent, Suppress and Punish Trafficking in Persons, Especially Women and Children.

concern with state policies at the national level (in this case, immigration policy) often overrides any humanitarian concern about the victims of cross-national crime, a set of priorities which can make such crime easier to perpetrate and get away with.

It is obvious how this applies to Alenka's case. But there is a more general point about criminal justice responding mainly to the activities of ordinary criminals and not recognising the social problems generated by corporate, white-collar and organised crime. Much of the political discourse – and most of the consequent policymaking – about criminal victimisation is blinkered by this failure to think of victims of white-collar crime and transnational organised crime[3] as victims in the same sense as someone who is burgled, robbed or has his or her property vandalised by an individual offender. As Punch (1996, p.253) has pointed out, 'criminal law is still predominantly shaped on individual behaviour and guilt; it is insufficiently geared to *organizational* forms of deviance'.

There can be little doubt that white-collar crime has victims, whether they are people of limited means who are tricked into paying their savings over to fraudsters, or workers killed as a result of corporate decisions to save money on health and safety. These 'crimes of the suits' attract far less attention – and fewer enforcement resources – than the street crime with which conventional discourse about crime is so preoccupied (Hillyard and Tombs 2004). Incidents in which people are killed through negligence tend to be characterised as accidents or disasters rather than treated as crime scenes, and many victims accept this: 'the majority of those suffering from corporate crime remain unaware of their victimization – either not knowing it has happened to them or viewing their "misfortune" as an accident' (Box 1983, p.17).

Regulatory procedures developed for dealing with corporate crime tend to favour negotiation rather than confrontation. Adversarial approaches to regulation in the business context are time-consuming and expensive, and often seen as counter-productive: conciliation works better from a commercial point of view according to some commentators, at least as long as punitive enforcement remains available in the reserve in the event of non-compliance. Attempting enforcement by negotiated means first also makes the more

---

3   This is a problematic term: those who have studied transnational crime point out that the phrase 'transnational organised crime' is misleading if it is interpreted as describing a purely external threat. Organised crime such as people-trafficking could not survive without its roots in the host countries, both in terms of the demand for young prostitutes and the UK-based offenders involved (Rawlinson 2002; see also Goodey 2005, Chapter 8).

coercive measures seem more legitimate when the time comes to use them (Punch 1996; Braithwaite 2002, Chapter 2 for a contrary view, see Slapper and Tombs 1999; Davis 2004; Tombs forthcoming). In practice, this approach can make it easier for businesses to conceal misconduct, not only because illegal behaviour may not be brought into the open or taken especially seriously, but also because superficial and temporary compliance may be sufficient to get the watchdog off the company's back, at least for the time being.

Punch gives the example of drug companies' deliberate misrepresentation of the benefits and side-effects of Thalidomide in Germany and the UK, and their subsequent obstruction of scientific and regulatory investigations. The cover-up led directly to an unknown number of deaths and the birth of many people with preventable disabilities (the drug had been explicitly sold, against all the evidence, as safe for pregnant women to take). Victims in some countries were put in the position of having to struggle to be defined as such. In the aftermath of the legal cases, the drug companies involved also obstructed victims' attempts to gain compensation, and conducted lengthy misinformation campaigns. In Germany a compensation fund was set up by the state, financed by the profits from sales of the drug. However, the UK company, Distillers,

> fought a very tough, penny-pinching campaign on compensation and only capitulated when the scandal began to hit them hard on the stock market and when politicians began to generate a sense of outrage in Parliament…the publicity was focused on the group of seriously deformed children; almost unnoticed and unreported was the battle for compensation for a second group of less severely deformed victims, and here the company tenaciously and ruthlessly fought for every penny. (Punch 1996, p.163)

Thalidomide was not an isolated example, but it is unlikely to be repeated in exactly the same way. The drug companies now tend to use consumers in Third World and Eastern European countries to test new drugs: 'the Thalidomide tragedy could be repeated, but most likely it would happen in a developing country' (Punch 1996, p.164; see also Tomlinson 2004). Victimisation is as subject to globalisation as other social phenomena, and the consequences are very serious for victims.

Another example of corruption arising from greed and the failure of regulation which led to large-scale victimisation was the unnecessary death and injury toll in the Turkish earthquake of 1999 (Green and Ward 2004, Chapter 4).

Over a period of time, 'building amnesties' had been corruptly granted by local planning authorities in an area well known to be susceptible to earthquakes. This encouraged builders to cut corners where safety was concerned and erect unsafe blocks of flats and hotels designed without consultation with costly architects or engineers. Not surprisingly, many such buildings collapsed in the earthquake. Much of the blame was publicly laid at the door of the building companies, but in some cases the same companies were then employed after the earthquake to replace the accommodation which had been demolished. Many of those living in the affected areas are Kurdish immigrants who had fled to the area to get away from the war in the south-east of the country. This underprivileged minority status no doubt made it more difficult to get their victimisation taken seriously by the authorities.

A more recent example in England also demonstrated the potential consequences for marginalised groups of victims: a new legal framework eventually had to be created to regulate the activities of 'gangmasters', criminal entrepreneurs who sell the labour of non-citizens, after 21 cockle-pickers died when they were cut off by the tide in the notoriously dangerous Morecambe Bay, where they had been taken to work collecting shellfish (Goodey 2005). The problem of the harvesting methods which were endangering and exploiting these workers was by no means unknown prior to the tragedy, and immigrant labour has routinely been exploited in the UK agriculture and shellfish industries for many years (HCEFRAC 2004a). Bonded labour, illegal deductions from pay, failure to pay the minimum wage, excessive working hours, crowded living accommodation, breaches of health and safety law and tax fiddles are all common (Lawrence 2004c). All the same, it took the large number of deaths in dramatic circumstances to highlight the issue at a political level. The combination of outlaw status for workers in the shadow economy who are trafficked illegally and dangerous working environments which are not properly regulated makes this kind of tragedy all but inevitable. The traffickers not only profit from smuggling their workers out of China, they go on to profit from providing poor quality accommodation and deducting the extortionate rents from earnings, and from paying illegally low wages. The workers are victims of forced labour in all but name, because they are in debt bondage to the gangmasters and many do not speak English (Lawrence 2004a; Yun 2004).

The police investigating the deaths were initially reluctant to label it a manslaughter or murder enquiry, speaking instead in terms of violations of tax, health and employment laws (Wainwright 2004). A number of people were arrested on suspicion of manslaughter (Press Association 2004), but the offence of corporate manslaughter exists only in very limited circumstances in the UK.[4] The Gangmasters (Licensing) Act 2004 became law only a few months after the tragedy and comes into force in 2006, having been put forward as a private member's bill (which is normally unlikely to result in legislative change: the bill in this case was supported by the government, after ministers were shamed into doing so by being criticised for failing to take any initiative on the issue: see Lawrence 2004b, Pye 2004; Yun 2004. The government had previously opposed anything other than a voluntary form of regulation in meetings with the relevant trade unions: see *Hazards Magazine* 2004). The legislation established a licensing scheme for 'labour providers' in the agricultural and shellfish farming industries, although as yet it remains unclear how effective this measure will prove to be in practice (for details of the legislation see www.defra.gov.uk). It is clearly only part of the response required by the authorities to prevent such tragedies occurring again in the future (HCEFRAC 2004a), and it arguably demonstrates the reactive nature of States' policies in this area. Only when faced by 'organised public resentment' do nation states legislate against the grain of their preference for negotiated approaches to health and safety enforcement (Pearce and Tombs 1997, p.93).

The costs of corporate and organised crime are undoubtedly borne disproportionately by those who are already disadvantaged in various ways (particularly in terms of class, race and gender: see Slapper and Tombs 1999). In the UK, enforcement measures are becoming less, rather than more, frequent and effective as regulatory bodies such as the Health and Safety Executive have their budgets cut and the emphasis changes from inspection and enforcement to voluntary codes of conduct in order to reduce the burdens of a range of forms of regulation upon businesses (Davis 2004; ETUTBHS 2004; *Hazards Magazine* 2004). Nevertheless, the government has recently allocated funding for extra staff to enforce gangmasters' observation of the tax laws (HCEFRAC 2004b), a measure which is concerned with maximising state income rather than protecting the workforce.

As long as crime policy – and criminology – ignore or downplay corporate crime, they are also likely to neglect to deal with its victims:

---

4   Although a corporate crime bill was promised in the government's 2001 manifesto, it was published only as a draft after its inclusion in the Queen's Speech for the final session of that parliament, when it had no hope of becoming law. The UK government has yet to sign the UN Convention on the Rights of all Migrant Workers and Members of their Families, signed or ratified by 42 other countries by the end of 2004.

the extent to which we are misled concerning the real nature of crime and criminal activity may lead to the support of policies which not only ignore the sources of victimization but may render that victimization worse. (Walklate 1989, p.107)

Part of the problem in exposing this kind of victimisation to view is the social distance which typically exists between the victimiser and the victim in the case of corporate and organised crime: the power differences between victim and offenders are even greater than is frequently the case in relation to 'street' crime, and it is often difficult to prove a causal chain of effect between the activities of the perpetrators and the suffering of the victims (Slapper and Tombs 1999). Even where the causal links are obvious, as in the case of transnational trafficking of women, the socially marginalised status of the victims and the ruthlessness of the perpetrators may render them powerless to assert their victim status.

Legislation designed to protect victims' rights can change this situation, as in some of the examples given above. The question of the definition of a victim of crime is important in this context. In England and Wales, the definition of a victim is left out of the relevant legislation (the Domestic Violence, Crime and Victims Act 2004): the minister responsible, the Home Secretary, is given the power (in section 32) to issue a Code of Practice for Victims including such definitions.[5] This could serve to pre-empt a public debate about who should be defined as victims (and although there is provision for a consultation period before the original draft Code comes into force, the Home Secretary can then amend it at will). There is a danger that this could allow political expediency to dictate the definition. In practice, as Rock (2004) has shown, the informal but highly influential Victims Steering Group convened by the Home Office has defined who is covered by policy on victims in the UK for 20 years. Victim Support is represented on this group, but no other victim support agencies have been invited to join it and this has influenced policy, not least in the comparative neglect of issues of the victimisation of women and children. It would be surprising if ruling politicians, given a choice, were to define victims of crime legally in ways which drew in the kinds of victims described in the first part of this chapter. It would be against their interests to

---

5   Strictly speaking, the Act does provide a definition, but it is so tautologous as to be meaningless: in section 52 (2) the Act states '"victim" means (a) a victim of an offence, or (b) a victim of anti-social behaviour'. The inclusion of the second clause suggests a wider definition than many might have expected.

do so, because it would raise awkward issues about compensation, liability and power.

Apart from the way in which victims are defined, the nature of any new rights granted to victims and witnesses is clearly important in assessing legislation and policy, as are the ways in which such legislation is actually implemented. Earlier in this book, the processes by which particular groups claim victim status and the obstacles which stand in their way have frequently been discussed. The emergence of an increasingly powerful victims' lobby has made it more difficult to ignore issues of policy which impinge upon victims in many wealthy countries, and in some poorer ones too. The concessions granted in the name of victims' rights and needs have often been tokenistic, however, and it is when considering the claims of emergent groups of victims that the State's reluctance to accommodate victims in legislative and policy provisions is most sharply highlighted.

Implications for future research

Hard to reach groups of victims, including the victims of hate crimes, people with learning difficulties and children, are under-researched at present. A few examples should suffice to illustrate this point.

The abuse of vulnerable adults in their own homes and in care institutions has only begun to receive official attention relatively recently, and even in those countries where awareness has increased and legislation has been passed, inter-agency adult protection work often neglects the victim perspective. Even in countries such as the UK, where official guidelines stipulate that victims should be fully involved in decision-making (or invited to appoint an advocate to represent their interests) (DoH 2004), this often does not happen in practice (Jeary 2004). Advocacy schemes which could assist in this way are few and far between, in any event. Thus, decisions are made about suspected victims of sexual or financial abuse without the victim's own views being directly represented. The size of the problem is not known and there is a clear need for further research into the position of victims of these kinds of offences (see Tarrant 2003, an article which includes several revealing case studies). People with learning difficulties are particularly vulnerable to sexual offending, especially if they live in institutional settings, and despite changes in the law to bring penalties into line with those for sexual offences against non-disabled people, allegations remain much less likely to be investigated and there are fewer prosecutions, of which fewer result in convictions. The question at issue is whether people with disabilities are believed in the same way as non-disabled people when they make complaints – and, indeed, whether they are equally valued as members of society.

Similarly, people with identifiable disabilities living in the community are frequently subjected to hate crimes and harassment, but the victim's perspective is rarely heard (Perry 2004). Incidents thoughtlessly described as 'bullying' often constitute criminal offences, and the persistence of such incidents can make life a misery for the victims (Williams 1999a). Hate crime, including crimes against people with disabilities, has legal standing in the USA, but not in many other countries. Recognition of the seriousness of this type of offending in terms of its impact upon the victims is only likely to come about if there is more evidence, and this area has been neglected by victimological research outside the USA with a very few exceptions (see Bowling 1999; Pritchard 2001; Tarrant 2003; Knight and Chouhan 2002; Perry 2004).

Although such offences receive little media attention, children have been killed by parents on a number of occasions as a result of contact, granted by courts, with non-custodial parents. According to Women's Aid, this is a serious problem in the UK: their anecdotal evidence suggests that 10 children were killed during contact arrangements during the three years from 2002 to 2004, and that contact arrangements are sometimes made by courts despite evidence that the partner applying for contact has a history of serious violence. Women's Aid has called for the introduction of a systematic way of assessing the risks involved in access cases (Women's Aid 2004). This is another good example of a group which is particularly prone to victimisation, children, and of special circumstances which appear to increase that risk, about which there has been little, if any, empirical research (see Boswell 2005).

Perhaps surprisingly, there are major aspects of the experience of women victims and offenders which remain under-researched. McIvor (2004) has pointed out that there is almost no research which distinguishes between women and men (or young men and women) as participants in restorative justice conferences. Experiences of victimisation are clearly gendered and victimology, of all disciplines, ought to be able to avoid designing and carrying out gender-blind research – but it does still happen (Walklate 2003). Researchers need to remain on guard against their own conditioning and assumptions, in this area as in many others. It is important to establish the ways in which women's experiences of restorative justice, and criminal justice in general, differ from those of male victims.

Another neglected issue in research terms is the indirect victimisation of police officers, victim support workers, jurors and others involved in assisting victims and hearing their stories. While victim support agencies generally have good systems of staff and volunteer supervision, these are not necessarily in place in other agencies working with victims, and the failure to provide such mechanisms potentially endangers the well-being of the people concerned. Even the best-resourced agencies can neglect staff welfare in this way: police liaison officers, for example, do not necessarily receive appropriate supervision or help when they get out of their depth, over-involved or particularly distressed by high-profile or very serious cases (Williams 1999a, p.101; Nuttall and Morrison 1997). Many people find jury service stressful, and a minority of jurors experience extreme and distressing psychological symptoms. Graphic descriptions and photographs of crime scenes and injuries can be profoundly disturbing to jurors and court officials. The criminal justice system fails to prepare them appropriately for this and, in the case of jurors, nobody even enquires about how they have found the experience. In this instance, the situation is further complicated by conventions about secrecy of the deliberations of juries: people are not sure whether they are allowed to talk about what upset them, even to family members. There is a need for independent research in this area, although the criminal justice system has traditionally obstructed research access to jurors. This may be partly because public awareness of the emotional and practical difficulties arising from jury service has led to an increased reluctance by members of the public to serve on juries. (Williams 2002).

As discussed in Chapter Three, surprisingly little is known about the connection between offenders' feelings of empathy towards victims and their future behaviour. While it is taken for granted in much of the literature about influencing offenders' behaviour that it must be a good thing to encourage and develop feelings of empathy, there is a lack of empirical evidence on this issue (see Van Stokkom 2002). Whether it is worthwhile to try to elicit victim empathy in offenders is a crucial question from the point of view of victim support agencies and individual victims, and it is an issue which requires a major research effort if it is to be thoroughly addressed. Some work has already been done in this area, and it reveals some gaps in existing knowledge.

Retzinger and Scheff (1996) observed a small number of restorative justice conferences in order to draw up good practice guidelines on how to achieve effective reintegrative shaming of offenders. They suggested that interactions between victims and offenders in this context could be managed in ways which facilitated reconciliation between the parties and changes in offenders' attitudes. Maxwell and Morris (2001) interviewed participants in family group conferences, and found that remorse on the part of young offenders and their parents seemed to be linked to reduced rates of re-offend-ing – but the study was a small one and the authors advised against making too much of their findings, suggesting that further research was required. As Morris subsequently put it, 'What we really need to know is how young people feel about what they have experienced and whether or not that impacts on their likelihood to re-offend' (2002b, p.173).

Part of the problem is that existing ways of assessing empathy are crude, and the psychological literature on shame, guilt and empathy is often vague about the meanings of and distinctions between these terms (see Proeve and Howells 2002). Matters are complicated by the likelihood that victims will also experience feelings of shame and guilt, and in the context of restorative justice they may also display empathy for the offender (Braithwaite and Mugford 1994; Braxton 2003/04). Conceptual issues require clarification and research instruments need development. Practitioners are clearly con-vinced of the benefits of restorative justice for offenders and victims and of the validity of trying to generate empathy on the part of offenders. Their col-laboration in the design and execution of appropriate research will be impor-tant in establishing whether, and in what circumstances, such confidence is justified. The involvement of victim support agencies in restorative initiatives such as family group conferences and referral panels depends crucially on their trust in the people running such programmes and on a belief that they are based upon a sound knowledge base.

It has become clear in this chapter that corporate crime, its handling, its victims and its investigation have traditionally been regarded as peripheral to criminology and victimology. If academic work on victims is to be compre-hensive, this will need to be addressed. To give only one example, little is cur-rently known about the contributory factors involved in people-trafficking (Egan and Millar 2004, p.11).

The enforcement of criminal penalties has an often unacknowledged importance for victims of crime, as discussed in Chapters One and Four. Research on enforcing the payment of fines and compensation has not so far paid much attention to victims' views, and it would be helpful to know what approaches to enforcement they regard as being in their best interests. Where the crimes of corporate bodies are concerned, the effects of requiring an industry to finance its own regulation would also repay further study: for example, while the chemical industry in the US state of New Jersey has accepted and co-operated with such an arrangements, little is known about the potential applications of such an approach in other contexts (Pearce and Tombs 1997), although Braithwaite (2002) has begun to bring together what has been learnt about internalising the costs of regulation in the corporate sector and its possible implications for restorative justice. If large companies can be persuaded to pay for the enforcement of health and safety regulations, this may have important implications for other areas of enforcement.

Louise Ellison's research (2001), which was mentioned in Chapters One and Four, has demonstrated the need for further investigation of a number of issues related to witnesses and the ways in which they are permitted to give evidence in court. Many of the conventional safeguards of defendants' rights have a questionable or counter-productive effect in terms of enabling witnesses to give good evidence. In particular, Ellison (2001, p.31) has argued that while the rules have been modified to make this easier for certain vulnerable witnesses, 'the rules and procedures sustaining the orality principle operate to deny the courts access to the best evidence potentially available in many more cases'. The principle that witnesses should normally give evidence in person and be cross-examined in front of the accused and – where applicable – the jury, is an ancient one based on a belief that people are more likely to tell the truth if they are in front of an audience and directly accountable to the judge and lawyers, but this has no basis in psychological research. Moreover, Ellison's research shows that vulnerable witnesses are likely to give their best evidence if it is videotaped while the incident is still fresh in their minds, as they routinely can in some parts of Australia.

This has the added advantage that lawyers are much less likely to try to discredit victims and witnesses 'on the basis of stereotypical perceptions as to how "real" victims should react to their experience', for example of sexual offences (Ellison 2001, p.132). Ellison's work raises a range of important issues which merit further investigation. The implementation of the special measures introduced by the Youth Justice and Criminal Evidence Act is being researched for the Home Office, but this will not answer questions in relation to the orality principle in general. If vulnerable witnesses can give better evidence as a result of special measures, why should these be denied to others whose evidence is needed? Indeed, might there not be better alternatives to the adversarial trial process from the point of view of victims and witnesses? As Ellison (2001, p.160) concludes:

> The ultimate test of the government's declared commitment to meeting the needs and interests of victims of crime and witnesses more generally will be a preparedness to move beyond the straitjacket of established trial procedure in the search for solutions.

As knowledge about the experiences of witnesses in court grows, the current legal conventions become increasingly difficult to sustain, but centuries of legal tradition will be difficult to supplant. There will be a need for rigorous research not only into the working of the new arrangements for special measures for vulnerable witnesses, but also more generally, into the best ways to enable witnesses to give the most useful evidence that they can.

It is clear from the discussion of compensation in Chapter Four that its availability can be beneficial to victims if it is properly administered – but that there are serious practical problems with delivering it effectively. However, there is a remarkable lack of recent research about compensation and victims' views on receiving financial restitution – particularly in view of the rise of interest in restorative justice (Mair 2004). In many criminal justice systems, financial penalties play a very substantial part in the repertoire of sentencing options (although, as Mair points out, their use has diminished substantially in England and Wales over the past decade, for reasons which are poorly understood). For a variety of reasons, it might be beneficial to increase the use made of compensation orders – but further research about the impact upon victims is certainly required. At present, it is unclear whether victims are satisfied by fines and compensation orders in relatively minor cases, and courts need this information if their confidence in making extensive use of financial penalties is to be restored.

Action research (that is, evaluative research which is intended to influence future policy, and in which the researchers provide interim findings in a dynamic relationship with the research subjects and commissioners) is one way of assessing the viability of new approaches to working with victims of crime. This approach has long been favoured by Victim Support and other victim service agencies in the UK (see, for example, the discussion of the Witness Service in Chapter Five). Encouragingly, it has also recently been employed by the Home Office. One example is the development of the conditional caution, which is a formal police warning given to minor offenders rather than prosecuting them, on condition that they complete certain activities as part of the caution or else face prosecution. This new type of police caution was introduced by the 2003 Criminal Justice Act, and it has been piloted in a number of police areas prior to a decision about its implementation nationally. In order to test the applicability of restorative justice approaches to conditional cautioning, the six pilot projects are designed to use such approaches in some areas but not in others, so as to facilitate comparisons. Restorative processes can be used to decide upon the conditions to be attached to cautions in some police areas, or restorative justice activities such as reparation can form conditions. On a larger scale, the government has also funded randomised control trials of a variety of restorative interventions in criminal justice during the period 2002 to 2007. Importantly, this research will include seeking information on levels of victims' satisfaction with the service they received (Nelson 2004).

Much of the research reviewed in this book demonstrates the need to ask victims themselves about the experience of victimisation and of becoming a user of criminal justice services – and a remarkable proportion of victimological research fails to talk to victims. Whole new services are created for victims without their voices being heard: 'victim-centred justice programmes often evolve without or with very little direct critical impact from victims' (Goodey 2005, p.117). It is not sufficient to use the professionals who work with victims as a proxy for hearing victims' own views: professionals are bound to have preconceptions and vested interests in particular points of view. Of course, victims may well tell researchers things that they and those commissioning the research do not want to hear – but it was only when people began to hear these messages that services for victims came to be adapted to make them victim-friendlier. As Goodey goes on to point out, restorative justice researchers have moved increasingly towards evaluating services at least partly on the basis of measures of victim satisfaction, an approach which should be applied much more widely by victimologists. The whole criminal justice system should be evaluated in terms of its acceptability to victims. Evaluative research can provide indicators of best practice in different victim services, always bearing in mind the dangers of trying to apply the lessons learnt in one place to the different circumstances in another.

Implications for future policy and practice

How genuine is the apparent policy interest in victims? How can those other than 'ideal' victims best be served? These questions demonstrate the size of the task of shifting political rhetoric about victims away from victim-blaming attitudes (which were perpetuated by much of the early work in victimology: see Mawby and Walklate 1994; Williams 1999a, pp.16–20) and from the notion of 'rebalancing' justice as between the interests of offenders and victims. What victimological research has so far failed to achieve is to influence policymakers significantly in this way, although it is not for the want of trying (see, for example, Cape 2004; Goodey 2005).

There is a need for central government to find ways of working with a range of victims' organisations – not only those serving the 'ideal' victim and not only those which are content placidly to accept government's interpretations of victims' needs and rights. While the more radical victim support agencies may be perceived as a thorn in the flesh of justice ministries around the world, they nevertheless serve vital functions. Indeed, they are often consulted about policy proposals even by governments which provide them with no on-going funding. The treatment of Rape Crisis by the UK government is an illuminating case in point. Rape Crisis formed itself into a national federation in 1996 with the help of a grant from a charitable foundation. For the first time, consistent training and staff support became available to local centres, and they also worked with the federation as a network collecting information on the prevalence of rape and sexual assault and responding to government initiatives and consultations. From 2001, the government provided funding for the work of the federation, but when this expired in 2003 it was not renewed and the federation had to shut down. There is a possibility that further funding might become available through the Victims Fund created by the 2004 Domestic Violence, Crime and Victims Act, but the services of the federation have nevertheless been unavailable for a considerable period (Jones and Westmarland 2004). Whatever the reasons, the decision to cut the grant appears to represent a breakdown in relationships between the Home Office and the Rape Crisis movement which might have been avoided had the government sufficiently recognised the merits of the work undertaken by Rape Crisis both nationally and locally. It is to the government's credit that it introduced such funding for the first time in 2001, but short-term grants do little to secure the future of non-governmental organisations working with victims. Other victim service agencies outside the mainstream also struggle for financial survival and lack long-term funding. For example, Women's Aid has called for a long-term funding framework to ensure that services can be provided continuously and consistently across the UK (Women's Aid 2004). Similar pressures undoubtedly constrain effective victim support in other countries too.

Because of funding constraints, victim support agencies have limited if any capacity for outreach work. They are to some extent campaigning organisations, and because they are closely in touch with the day-to-day experiences of victims, they tend to find at least some time and resources for political action. However, as discussed in Chapter One, there is a delicate balance to be struck. In the UK, charitable organisations are legally restricted in terms of campaigning activities, and in any case they often have reasons to avoid antagonising the government of the day. There is scope for considerably more educational work based on organisations' experience garnered from direct work with victims. This would help to prevent victimisation in future. A different kind of outreach work might involve proactive efforts to publicise the services available: while public consciousness of victim service agencies is improving, it could certainly be increased significantly. Only a small minority of criminal offences result in a conviction, and much of the work of the service agencies, in the UK and elsewhere, is generated by referrals from a single source, the police. Victim Support and other agencies such as Rape Crisis and Women's Aid could clearly benefit from being able to spend more money on publicity, education and outreach work.

Limited funding also constrains the extent to which victim support organisations can liaise effectively with other agencies and provide for victims' practical needs. Policy attention to date has focused upon the criminal justice system, but victims' needs can go unmet because of the lack of victim awareness and responsiveness in health services, housing agencies and social security offices. Victim Support in England has, in recent years, widened its campaigning activities to draw attention to some of these deficiencies (Victim Support 2004b). Meanwhile, such agencies continue to undertake action research and demonstration projects, designed to demonstrate that newly identified needs can be met if funding is made available. Victim Support, for example, is involved in pilot projects providing support to people bereaved and seriously injured in road accidents and in separate projects providing support to child victims (who have traditionally been formally excluded from Victim Support's work due to concerns about the level of volunteer training required to do such work effectively).

The brief discussion, towards the end of Chapter Four, of cultural differences in attitudes towards service provision for victims of crime showed that international conventions and exhortations from international bodies will not be especially influential if they do not reflect the political and economic realities in the countries concerned. In some places, victim services will be slow to develop because they are a relatively low priority in poor countries where more basic needs go unmet. Elsewhere, the favoured model for providing support may differ from those of the drafters of international agreements. The case of Spain is an interesting one: although it is a rich, developed country, relatively little service provision has developed there in response to European and UN initiatives (CEC 2004). Only recently did victim compensation from state sources become available (usually the first policy initiative to be taken by nations in response to victims' needs), and the legal protection theoretically available to victims and witnesses is often not implemented in reality: 'implementation of the law still lags behind. It is therefore high time that the courts bring the law to life' (Brienen and Hoegen 2000, p.876).

In Spain, the impetus towards implementing and strengthening laws and policies in relation to victims of crime came partly from the Madrid train bombs in 2004 and the subsequent fall of the government as a result of its prevarication in response to the bombings. The new government appears to be much more committed to improving the experiences of victims and witnesses of crime, and has begun to commit substantial funding to initiatives intended to achieve this end. International collaboration has enjoyed renewed support, as Spain seeks expertise from elsewhere. Regional victims' associations and the national association for victims of terrorism have become more newsworthy, and they have taken the opportunity to press the case both for timely compensation and for other measures in response to the needs of victims of crime generally. Progress will probably be slow, as it so often is when building the case for an official response to a new demand for expenditure, but the issues have certainly been placed on the agenda. Similarly, the Dutroux case in Belgium led to enormous changes in the criminal justice system, including the restorative justice initiatives in prisons described in Chapter Five. While it is difficult to see the connection between a botched murder investigation and restorative justice in prison, there is a link: public dissatisfaction with the operation of the criminal justice system permitted system officials to begin to think 'outside the box', and once they did so, they looked further afield than they were used to doing. Dissatisfaction with the treatment of victims and their families led to a willingness to take new approaches. A closed, even corrupt criminal justice culture began to open up. At such times, innovation can occur.

When confronted with real victims and the ways in which criminal justice has failed them, politicians and public can discard preconceptions about the ideal victim and find ways to address victims' needs. Victimological research contributed to the stereotyping of 'the victim', at least in its initial approaches to researching victims, but it has now engaged effectively with victims themselves, and with victim services, to identify a positive agenda for future work. If it can also engage successfully with the policymakers who commission and (sometimes) act upon research, victims' voices are likely, increasingly, to be heard in the corridors of power.

References

Abramovsky, A. (1992) 'Victim impact statements: Adversely impacting upon judicial fairness', *St John's Journal of Legal Commentary*, pp.21–33.

Ahmed, K. (2002) 'Blair pledge to wage new crime war', *The Observer*, 10 November.

Akester, K. (2002) 'Restorative justice, victims' rights and the future', *Legal Action*, January, pp.1–4.

Alinsky, S. (1972) *Rules for Radicals*, New York: Vintage Press.

Altschuler, D. (2001) 'Community justice initiatives: Issues and challenges in the US context', *Federal Probation*, 65 (1) pp.28–32.

Angle, H., Malam, S. and Carey, C. (2003) *Witness Satisfaction: Findings from the Witness Satisfaction Survey 2002*, Home Office Online Report 19/03, London: Home Office, www.homeoffice.gov.uk/rds/pdts2/r189.pdt

Arrigo, B. R. and Williams, C. R. (2003) 'Victim vices, victim voices, and impact statements: On the place of emotion and the role of restorative justice in capital sentencing', *Crime and Delinquency*, 49 (4), pp.603–26.

Ashworth, A. (1993) 'Victim Impact Statements and sentencing', *Criminal Law Review*, pp.498–509.

Ashworth, A. (2000) 'Victims' rights, defendants' rights and criminal procedure', in Crawford, A. and Goodey, J. (eds) *Integrating a Victim Perspective within Criminal Justice*, Aldershot: Ashgate.

Ashworth, A. (2002) 'Responsibilities, rights and restorative justice', *British Journal of Criminal Justice*, 42 (3) pp.578–95.

Bailey, R. and Williams, B. (2000) *Inter-Agency Partnership in Youth Justice: Implementing the Crime and Disorder Act 2000*, Sheffield: Social Service Monographs.

Bates, A., Falshaw, L., Corbett, C., Patel, V. and Friendship, C. (2004) 'A follow-up study of sex offenders treated by Thames Valley Sex Offender Groupwork Programme, 1995–1999', *Journal of Sexual Aggression*, 10 (1) pp.29–38.

Bazemore, G. and Schiff, M. (2004) 'Paradigm muddle or paradigm paralysis? The wide and narrow roads to restorative justice reform (or, a little confusion may be a good thing)', *Contemporary Justice Review*, 7 (1) March, pp.37–57.

BBC News (2004) 'Speeding drivers face victim levy', Monday 12 January, www.speedcamerasuk.com/Media.htm

Bell, S. (2003) 'Extracts from an evaluation study', in QPSW, *Circles of Support and Accountability in the Thames Valley, Interim Report November 2003*, London: Quaker Peace and Social Witness.

Biermans, N. (2002) 'Restorative justice and the prison system', paper given at the European Conference on Victim–Offender Mediation, Ostend, Belgium, October (available from nadia.biermans@just.fgov.be).

Black, D. (1987) 'Compensation and the social structure of misfortune', *Law and Society Review*, 21 (4) pp.563–84.

Blagg, H. (1997) 'A just measure of shame? Aboriginal youth and conferencing in Australia', *British Journal of Criminology*, 37 (4) pp.481–501.

Blagg, H. (1998) 'Restorative visions and restorative justice practices: Conferencing, ceremony and reconciliation in Australia', *Current Issues in Criminal Justice*, 10 (1) pp.5–14.

Boswell, G. (2005) 'Child victims', *British Journal of Community Justice*, 3 (2) pp.9–23.

Bottoms, A. (2004) 'Empirical research relevant to sentencing frameworks', in Bottoms, A., Rex, S. and Robinson, G. (eds) *Alternatives to Prison: Options for an Insecure Society*, Cullompton: Willan.

Boutellier, H. (2000) *Crime and Morality: The Significance of Criminal Justice in Post-Modern Culture*, London: Kluwer Academic.

Bowling, B. (1999) *Violent Racism: Victimisation, Policing and Social Context*, Oxford: Oxford University Press.

Box, S. (1983) *Power, Crime and Mystification*, London: Tavistock.

Braithwaite, J. (1989) *Crime, Shame and Reintegration*, Cambridge: Cambridge University Press.

Braithwaite, J. (2000) 'The new regulatory state and the transformation of criminology', *British Journal of Criminology*, 40 (2) pp.228–38.

Braithwaite, J. (2002) *Restorative Justice and Responsive Regulation*, Oxford: Oxford University Press.

Braithwaite, J. and Daly, K. (1994) 'Masculinities, violence and communitarian control', in Newburn, T. and Stanko, E. A. (eds) *Just Boys Doing Business? Men, Masculinities and Crime*, London: Routledge.

Braithwaite, J. and Mugford, S. (1994) 'Conditions of successful reintegration ceremonies: Dealing with juvenile offenders', *British Journal of Criminology*, 34 (2), pp.139–71.

Braxton, H. (2003/04) 'Empathic encounter: The relationship between self-reported empathy, process, and outcome in a restorative justice program', *VOMA Connections*, 16, pp.1, 6, 8, 10–12.

Brienen, M. E. I. and Hoegen, E. H. (2000) *Victims of Crime in 22 European Criminal Justice Systems*, Nijmegen: Wolf Legal Productions.

Brimacombe, H. (2004) 'Bringing justice closer to the community', *Legal Action*, December, pp.10–11.

Buonatesta, A. (2004) 'La médiation entre auteurs et victimes dans le cadre de l'exécution de la peine', *Revue de Droit Pénal et de Criminologie*, February, pp.242–57.

Burton, S., Regan, L. and Kelly, L. (1998) *Supporting Women and Challenging Men: Lessons from the Domestic Violence Intervention Project*, Bristol: Policy Press.

Cain, M. (2000) 'Orientalism, occidentalism and the sociology of crime', *British Journal of Criminology*, 40 (2) pp.239–60.

Cape, E. (2004) (ed.) *Reconciliation Rights? Analysing the Tension between Victims and Defendants*. London: Legal Action Group.

Casey, C. (1999) 'Restoring the faith', *Policing Today*, March pp.36–8.

Cavadino, M. and Dignan, J. (2002) *The Penal System: An Introduction*, third edition, London: Sage.

CEC (2004) 'Document de travail des services de la Commission: Annexe au rapport de la Commission fondé sur l'article 18 de la décision-cadre du Conseil du 15 mars 2001 relative au statut des victimes dans la cadre des procédures pénales', COM (2004) 54 final, Brussels, Commission des Communautés Européennes.

Center for Sex Offender Management (2004) *Public Opinion and the Criminal Justice System: Building Support for Sex Offender Management Programs*, Silver Spring, MD: CSOM http://www.csom.org/pubs/pubpinion.html

Christie, N. (1977) 'Conflicts as property', *British Journal of Criminology*, 17 (1) pp.1–15, reproduced as Chapter 1 of McLaughlin, E., Fergusson, R., Hughes, G. and Westmarland, L. (eds) *Restorative Justice: Critical Issues*, London: Sage.

Christie, N. (1986) 'The ideal victim', in Fattah, E. A. (ed.) *From Crime Policy to Victim Policy: Reorienting the Justice System*, New York: St. Martin's Press.

Christie, N. (2000) *Crime Control as Industry: Towards Gulags, Western Style*, third edition, London: Routledge.

Christie, N. (2004) *A Suitable Amount of Crime*, London: Routledge.

CICA (2001) *A Guide to the Criminal Injuries Compensation Scheme (2001)*, Glasgow: Criminal Injuries Compensation Authority.

CICP (1999) *Handbook on Justice for Victims*, New York: United Nations Office for Drug Control and Crime Prevention, Centre for International Crime Prevention.

Clark, L. (2003) 'A volunteer's perspective (1)', in QPSW, *Circles of Support and Accountability in the Thames Valley, Interim Report November 2003*, London: Quaker Peace and Social Witness.

Clark, P. (2004) 'Redressing the balance: The Criminal Justice Bill 2002', in Cape, E. (ed.) *Reconcilable Rights? Analysing the Tension between Victims and Defendants*, London: Legal Action Group.

Clear, T. and Karp, D. R. (1998) 'The community justice movement', in Karp, D. R. (ed.) *Community Justice: An Emerging Field*, Oxford: Rowman and Littelfield.

Clear, T. R. and Karp, D. R. (2000) 'Toward the ideal of community justice', *National Institute of Justice Journal*, October, pp.20–28.

Collin, B. and Guffens, H. (undated) 'Trois ans de justice réparatrice dans nos prisons' (available from Hilde Guffens, Federal Department of Justice, Brussels, Belgium: hilde.guffens2@just.fgov.be)

Community Justice Initiatives (2004) *Community Justice Initiatives Annual Report 2003*, Langley, BC: CJI, available at http://www.cjibc.org

Consedine, J. (1995) *Restorative Justice: Healing the Effects of Crime*, Christchurch: Ploughshares.

Crawford, A. (1998) *Crime Prevention and Community Safety: Politics, Policies and Practices*, Harlow: Longman.

Crawford, A. and Enterkin, J. (1999) *Victim Contact Work and the Probation Service: A Study of Service Delivery and Impact*, Leeds: University of Leeds Centre for Criminal Justice Studies.

Crawford, A. and Newburn, T. (2003) *Youth Offending and Restorative Justice: Implementing Reform in Youth Justice*, Cullompton: Willan.

Crime Reduction website (2003) 'Liverpool to pioneer one-stop crime busting centre', press release, 10 September, www.crimereduction.gov.uk/criminaljusticesystem7.htm

Crown Prosecution Service (2004) *No Witness: No Justice, the National Victim and Witness Care Programme*, York: CPS.

CSC (Correctional Service Canada) (2001) *Circles of Support and Accountability: Evaluation Report*, Ottawa: CSC and at www.csc-scc.gc.ca/text/prgrm/chap/circles_support_e.shtml

Cunneen, C. (2003) 'Thinking critically about restorative justice', in McLaughlin, E., Fergusson, R., Hughes, G. and Westmarland, L. (eds) *Restorative Justice: Critical Issues*, London: Sage.

Curry, D., Knight, V., Owens-Rawle, D., Patel, S., Semenchuk, M. and Williams, B. (2004) *Restorative Justice in the Secure Estate*, London: Youth Justice Board.

Curtol, F., Decarli, S., Di Nicola, A. and Savona, E. U. (2004) 'Victims of human trafficking in Italy: A judicial perspective', *International Review of Victimology*, 11, pp.111–41.

Daly, K. (2000) 'Revisiting the relationship between retributive and restorative justice', in Strang, H. and Braithwaite, J. (eds) *Restorative Justice: From Philosophy to Practice*, Aldershot: Dartmouth.

Daly, K. (2002) 'Restorative justice: The real story', *Punishment and Society*, (4) 1 pp.55–79, reproduced as Chapter 16 in McLaughlin, E., Fergusson, R., Hughes, G. and Westmarland, L. (eds) (2003) *Restorative Justice: Critical Issues*, London: Sage.

Davis, C. (2004) *Making Companies Safe: What Works?*, London: Centre for Corporate Accountability.

Davis, R. C., Henderson, N. J. and Rabbitt, C. (2002) *Effects of State Victim Rights Legislation on Local Criminal Justice Systems*, New York: Vera Institute of Justice.

Dawson, M. and Dinovitzer, R. (2001) 'Victim cooperation and the prosecution of domestic violence in a specialized court', *Justice Quarterly*, 18 (3), September, pp.593–622.

Department of Constitutional Affairs (2004) advertisement for appointment of Community Justice Judge, Liverpool, http://www.dca.gov.uk/judicial/appointments/cjjl04/ccjladv04.htm

Department of Health (2004) *No Secrets: Guidance on Developing and Implementing Multi-Agency Policies and Procedures to Protect Vulnerable Adults from Abuse*, London: Department of Health.

Dignan, J. (2000) *Youth Justice Pilots Evaluation: Interim Reports on Reparative Work and Youth Offending Teams*, London: Home Office.

Dignan, J. (2002) 'Reparation orders', in Williams, B. (ed.) *Reparation and Victim-Focused Social Work*, London: Jessica Kingsley Publishers.

Dignan, J. (2005) *Understanding Victims and Restorative Justice*, Maidenhead: Open University Press.

DJELR (Department of Justice, Equality and Law Reform) (1999) *Victim's Charter and Guide to the Criminal Justice System*, Dublin: DJELR (www.justice.ie).

Dobash, R. E., Dobash, R. P., Cavanagh, K. and Lewis, R. (2000) *Changing Violent Men*, London: Sage.

Doble, J. (2002) 'Attitudes to punishment in the US – punitive and liberal opinions', in Roberts, J. V. and Hough, M. (eds) *Changing Attitudes to Punishment: Public Opinion, Crime and Justice*, Cullompton: Willan.

Doerner, W. G. and Lab, S. P. (2002) *Victimology*, third edition, Cincinnati, OH: Anderson.

Dolowitz, D., Greenwold, S. and Marsh, D. (1999) 'Policy transfer: Something old, something new, something borrowed, but why red, white and blue?', *Parliamentary Affairs*, 52, pp.719–30.

Dominey, J. (2002) 'Addressing victim issues in Pre-Sentence Reports', in B. Williams (ed.) *Reparation and Victim-Focused Social Work*, London: Jessica Kingsley Pubishers.

Drewery, H. (2003) 'Introduction', in QPSW, *Circles of Support and Accountability in the Thames Valley, Interim Report November 2003*, London: Quaker Peace and Social Witness.

Eadie, T. and Knight, C. (2002) 'Domestic violence programmes: Reflections on the shift from independent to statutory provision', *Howard Journal of Criminal Justice*, 41 (2) pp.167–81.

Edelhertz, H. and Geitz, G. (1974) *Public Compensation to Victims of Crime*, New York: Praeger.

Edwards, I. (2002) 'The place of victims' preferences in the sentencing of "their" offenders', *Criminal Law Review*, September, pp.689–702.

Egan, R. and Millar, L. (2004) 'The criminal exploitation of women and children trafficked into the United Kingdom', paper given at the International Police Executive Symposium Eleventh Annual Meeting, Vancouver, 16–20 May.

Eliaerts, C. and Dumortier, E. (2001) 'Restorative justice for children: In need of procedural safeguards and standards', in Weitekamp, E. G. M. and Kerner, H.-J. (eds) *Restorative Justice: Theoretical Foundations*, Cullompton: Willan.

Elias, R. (1984) *Victims of the System*, New Brunswick, NJ: Transaction.

Elias, R. (1993) *Victims Still: The Political Manipulation of Crime Victims*, London: Sage.

Ellison, L. (2001) *The Adversarial Process and the Vulnerable Witness*, Oxford: Oxford University Press.

Erez, E. (1999) 'Who's afraid of the big bad victim? Victim Impact Statements as victim empowerment *and* enhancement of justice', *Criminal Law Review*, July, pp.545–56.

Erez, E. (2004) 'Integrating restorative justice principles in adversarial proceedings through victim impact statements', in Cape, E. (ed.) *Reconcilable Rights? Analysing the Tension between Victims and Defendants*, London: Legal Action Group.

Erez, E., Ibarra, P.R. and McDonald, W. F. (2004) 'Transnational sex trafficking: Issues and prospects', *International Review of Victimology*, 11, pp.1–9.

Erez, E. and Rogers, L. (1999) 'The effects of Victim Impact Statements on criminal justice outcomes and processes: The perspectives of legal professionals', *British Journal of Criminology*, 39 (2) pp.216–39.

Erez, E. and Tontodonato, P. (1992) 'Victim participation in sentencing and satisfaction with justice', *Justice Quarterly*, 9, pp.393–417.

ETUTBHS (2004) 'UK: What works? Government's safety policies inconsistent with research', European Trade Union Technical Bureau for Health and Safety: http://tutb.etuc.org/uk/newsevents/newsfiche.asp?pk=182

Etzioni, A. (1994) *The Spirit of Community: The Reinvention of American Society*, New York: Touchstone.

Etzioni, A. (1995) (ed.) *New Communitarian Thinking*, London: University Press of Virginia.

Etzioni, A. (1998) 'Community justice in a communitarian perspective', in Karp, D. R. (ed.) *Community Justice: An Emerging Field*, Oxford: Rowman and Littelfield.

European Union Council of Justice and Home Affairs (2001) *Standing of Victims in Criminal Proceedings*, Luxembourg: Office for Official Proceedings of the European Communities.

Faulkner, D. (1994) 'Relational justice: A dynamic for reform' in Burnside, J. and Baker, N. (eds) *Relational Justice: Repairing the Breach*, Winchester: Waterside Press.

Faulkner, D. (2001) *Crime, State and Citizen: A Field Full of Folk*, Winchester: Waterside Press.

Findlay, M. (2000a) 'Decolonising restoration and justice in transitional cultures', in Strang, H. and Braithwaite, J. (eds) *Restorative Justice: Philosophy and Practice*, Aldershot: Ashgate.

Findlay, M. (2000b) 'Decolonising restoration and justice: Restoration in transitional cultures', *Howard Journal*, 39 (4) pp.398–411.

Fitzgerald, M. and Sim, J. (1982) *British Prisons*, second edition, Oxford: Basil Blackwell.

Freeman-Longo, R. E. (2000) 'Revisiting Megan's Law and sex offender registration: Prevention or problem', published on the American Probation and Parole Association website, http://www.appa-net.org/revisitingmegan.pdf

Fry, M. (1951) *Arms of the Law*, London: Howard League/Victor Gollancz.

Fry, M. (1957) 'Justice for victims', *The Observer*, 7 July.

Fursland, E. (2004) 'Circles of life', *The Guardian*, Society supplement, 28 January, http://society.guardian.co.uk/bestpractice/story/o,14091,1132201,00.html

Garland, D. (2001) *The Culture of Control: Crime and Social Order in Contemporary Society*, Oxford: Oxford University Press.

Gibb, J. (2003) 'Sex and slavery', *Observer Magazine*, 25 February, pp.24–29.

Gilberti, C. (1991) 'Evaluation of Victim Impact Statement projects in Canada: A summary of findings', in Kaiser, G. (ed) *Victims and Criminal Justice*, Freiburg, Germany: Max-Planck-Institut für Ausländisches und Internationales Strafrecht, pp.703–18.

Goodey, J. (2000) 'An overview of key themes', in Crawford, A. and Goodey, J. (eds) *Integrating a Victim Perspective within Criminal Justice*, Dartmouth: Ashgate.

Goodey, J. (2004) 'Promoting "good practice" in sex trafficking cases', *International Review of Victimology*, 11, pp.89–110.

Goodey, J. (2005) *Victims and Victimology: Research, Policy and Practice*, Harlow: Longman.

govnet (2004) 'Meeting the needs of reluctant witnesses', government press release, 13 December, www.govnet.co.uk/newsfeed.php?ID=5361

Graef, R. (2000) *Why Restorative Justice? Repairing the Harm Done by Crime*, London: Calouste Gulbenkian Foundation.

Green, P. and Ward, T. (2004) *State Crime: Governments, Violence and Corruption*, London: Pluto.

Greene, J. and Doble, J. (2000) *Attitudes Towards Crime and Punishment in Vermont: Public Opinion about an Experiment with Restorative Justice*, Rockville, MD: NCJRS: available at http://www.ncjrs.org

Gustafson, D. L. and Smidstra, H. (1989) *Victim Offender Reconciliation in Serious Crime: A Report on the Feasibility Study Undertaken for the Ministry of the Solicitor General*, Ottawa: Solicitor General Canada.

Hamlyn, B., Phelps, A., Turtle, J. and Sattar, G. (2004) *Are Special Measures Working? Evidence from Surveys of Vulnerable and Intimidated Witnesses*, Research Study 283, London: Home Office Research, Development and Statistics Directorate.

Hansard (2004) House of Commons Debates for 27 October, www.publications.parliament.uk/pa/cm200304/cmhansard/cm041027/debindx/41027-x.htm

Hartless, J. M., Ditton, J., Mair, G. and Phillips, S. (1995) 'More sinned against than sinning: A study of young teenagers' experience of crime', *British Journal of Criminology*, 35 (1) pp.114–33.

Hazards Magazine (2004) 'Who's protecting the migrant workers?', website feature, www.hazards.org/migrants/

HCEFRAC (2004a) *Gangmasters (Follow Up), Eighth Report of Session 2003–2004*, HC 455, House of Commons Environment, Food and Rural Affairs Committee, London: Stationery Office.

HCEFRAC (2004b) *Minutes of Evidence, Supplementary Memorandum Submitted by the Government*, House of Commons Environment, Food and Rural Affairs Committee, London: House of Commons, www.publications.parliament.uk/pa/cm200304/cmselect/cmenvfru/550/4050401.htm

Heise, E., Horne, L., Kierkegaard, H., Nigh, H., Derry, I. and Yantzi, M. (2000) *Community Reintegration Project: Circles of Support and Accountability*, Ottawa: Correctional Services Canada.

Her Majesty's Inspectorate of Probation (2003) *Valuing the Victim: An Inspection into National Victim Contact Arrangements*, London: Home Office.

Hickman, J. (2004) 'Playing games and cheating: Fairness in the criminal justice system' in Cape, E. (ed.) *Reconcilable Rights? Analysing the Tension between Victims and Defendants*, London: Legal Action Group.

Hillyard, P. and Tombs, S. (2004) 'Beyond criminology?', in Hillyard, P., Pantazis, C., Tombs, S. and Gordon, D. (eds) *Beyond Criminology: Taking Harm Seriously*, London: Pluto.

Hinton, M. (1995) 'Expectations dashed: Victim impact statements and the common law approach to sentencing in South Australia', *University of Tasmania Law Review*, 14, pp.81–99.

Home Office (undated) *The Victim Personal Statement: A Guide for Investigators*, London: Home Office, http://www.homeoffice.gov.uk/docs/guideinvestig.pdf

Home Office (1990) *Victim's Charter: A Statement of the Rights of Victims of Crime*, London: Home Office Public Relations Branch.

Home Office (1999) *The Role of Victims in the Criminal Justice Process: Conference Report*, Liverpool: Home Office Special Conferences Unit.

Home Office (2000) 'Domestic violence: Revised circular to the Police', Home Office Circular no. 19/2000, London: Home Office, www.homeoffice.gov.uk/docs/ hoc1900.html

Home Office (2001) *Criminal Justice: The Way Ahead*, Cm. 5074, London: Home Office.

Home Office (2003) *A New Deal for Victims and Witnesses: National Strategy to Deliver Improved Services*, London: Home Office.

Home Office (2004a) *Compensation and Support for Victims of Crime: Possible Changes to the Criminal Injuries Compensation Scheme*, London: Home Office.

Home Office (2004b) 'Domestic Violence, Crime and Victims Bill receives royal assent', press release ref. 353/2004, 15 November, www.homeoffice.gov.uk/ n_story.asp?item_id=1147

Home Office (2004c) *'Compensation and Support for Victims of Crime': Summary of Responses to a Home Office Consultation Paper*, http://www.cjsonline.gov.uk

Home Office, Crown Prosecution Service and Department for Constitutional Affairs (2004) *Best Practice Guidance to Form the Basis of Training and Accreditation*, London: Home Office and at http://www.homeoffice.gov.uk/justice/victims/restorative

Home Office and Scottish Home and Health Department (1964) *Compensation for Victims of Crime and Violence*, Cmnd. 2323, London: HMSO.

Home Office, Lord Chancellor's Department, Attorney General and Association of Chief Police Officers (2002) *Narrowing the Justice Gap*, London: Home Office Communications Directorate.

Hough, M. and Park, A. (2002) 'How malleable are attitudes to crime and punishment? Findings from a British deliberative poll', in Roberts, J. V. and Hough, M. (eds) *Changing Attitudes to Punishment: Public Opinion, Crime and Justice*, Cullompton: Willan.

Howard League for Penal Reform (1977) *Making Amends: Criminals, Victims and Society*, Chichester: Barry Rose.

Hoyle, C. (2002) 'Securing restorative justice for the "non-participating" victim', in Hoyle, C. and Young, R. (eds) *New Visions of Crime Victims*, Oxford: Hart.

Hoyle, C., Cape, E., Morgan, R. and Sanders, A. (1999) *Evaluation of the 'One Stop Shop' and Victim Statement Pilot Projects*, London: Home Office RDSD.

HSE (undated) 'Collecting witness evidence: Witness statements', London: Health and Safety Executive, www.hse.gov.uk/enforce/enforcementguide/investigation/witness/witness.htm

Hudson, B. (2004) 'Balancing the rights of victims and offenders', in Cape, E. (ed.) *Reconcilable Rights? Analysing the Tension between Victims and Defendants*, London: Legal Action Group.

Hughes, G. (1996) 'Communitarianism and law and order', *Critical Social Policy*, 49, pp.17–41.

Hughes, G. (2000) 'Crime and disorder reduction partnerships: The future of community safety?', in Hughes, G., McLaughlin, E. and Muncie, J. (eds) *Crime Prevention and Community Safety: New Directions*, London: Sage.

Hughes, G. (2001a) 'Community justice', in McLaughlin, E. and Muncie, J. (eds) *The Sage Dictionary of Criminology*, London: Sage, pp.40–1.

Hughes, G. (2001b) 'Communitarianism', in McLaughlin, E. and Muncie, J. (eds) *The Sage Dictionary of Criminology*, London: Sage, pp.35–7.

Hughes, G., McLaughlin, E. and Muncie, J. (eds) (2002) *Crime Prevention and Community Safety: New Directions*, London: Sage.

Jackson, J. (2004) 'Putting victims at the heart of criminal justice: The gap between rhetoric and reality', in Cape, E. (ed.) *Reconcilable Rights? Analysing the Tension between Victims and Defendants*, London: Legal Action Group, pp.65–79.

Jackson, S. (1998) *Family Justice? An Evaluation of the Hampshire Youth Justice Family Group Conferencing Project*, Southampton: University of Southampton.

Jeary, K. (2004) 'The victim's voice: How is it heard? Issues arising from adult protection case conferences', *Journal of Adult Protection*, 6 (1) pp.12–19.

Jenkins, P. (2002) 'Introduction' in Jenkins, P. (ed.) *Legal Issues in Counselling and Psychotherapy*, London: Sage.

JHSA (1997) *Victim Impact Statements*, Edmonton, Canada: John Howard Society of Alberta.

Johnstone, G. (2002) *Restorative Justice: Ideas, Values, Debates*, Cullompton: Willan.

Jones, H. and Westmarland, N. (2004) 'Rape Crisis history: Remembering the past but looking to the future', www.rapecrisis.org.uk/history.htm

Jordan, B. and Arnold, J. (1995) 'Democracy and criminal justice', *Critical Social Policy* 44/45, pp.170–82.

Justice (1998) *Victims in Criminal Justice: Report of the Justice Committee on the Role of the Victim in Criminal Justice*, London: Justice.

Karan, A., Keilitz, S. and Denaro, S. (1999) 'Domestic violence courts: What are they and how should we manage them?', *Juvenile and Family Court Journal*, Spring, pp.75–84.

Karp, D. R. (2002) 'The offender/community encounter: Stakeholder involvement in the Vermont Community Reparative Boards', in Karp, D. R. and Clear, T. R. (2002) (eds) *What is Community Justice? Case Studies of Restorative Justice and Community Supervision*, London: Sage.

Karp, D. R. (2004) 'Birds of a feather: A response to the McCold critique of community justice', *Contemporary Justice Review*, 7 (1) March, pp.59–67.

Karp, D. R. and Clear, T. R. (2002) (eds) *What is Community Justice? Case Studies of Restorative Justice and Community Supervision*, London: Sage.

Kilgallon, J. (2004) Interview with project manager, Warwickshire Victim and Witness Information Partnership, Leamington Spa, 19 August.

Knight, C. and Chouhan, K. (2002) 'Supporting victims of racist abuse and violence', in Williams, B. (ed.) *Reparation and Victim-Focused Social Work*, Research Highlights 42, London: Jessica Kingsley Publishers.

Kurki, L. (2000) 'Restorative and community justice in the United States', in Tonry, M. (ed.) *Crime and Justice: A Review of the Research*, 27, pp.235–303.

Latimer, J., Dowden, C. and Muise, D. (2001) *The Effectiveness of Restorative Justice Practices: A Meta-Analysis*, Ottawa: Research and Statistics Division, Department of Justice Canada.

Lawrence, F. (2004a) 'Chinese cockle-pickers – part I', *East South West North: Global Culture and Politics*, 9 February, http://www.zonaeuropa.com/01107.htm

Lawrence, F. (2004b) 'Ministers admit to not acting on illegal labour gangmasters', *The Guardian*, Society Supplement, 24 March, www.guardian.co.uk/asylumseekers/story/0,7991, 1176461,00.html.

Lawrence, F. (2004c) 'Labour laws breached, study finds' *The Guardian*, 17 November, p.12.

Leicestershire and Rutland Probation Area (2004) *Victims: A Strategy for Delivering Services to Victims and for Integrating Victims Issues into the Work of Leicestershire and Rutland Probation Area 2004–2005*, Leicester: LRPA.

Lobley, D. and Smith, D. (2003) *The Witness Service Five Years On: An Evaluation in 2003*, Edinburgh: Scottish Executive Social Research.

Macpherson, W. (1999) *The Stephen Lawrence Inquiry Report*, Cm. 4262, London: HMSO.

Maguire, M. and Kynch, J. (2000) *Public Perceptions and Victims' Experiences of Victim Support: Findings from the 1998 British Crime Survey*, London: Home Office Research, Development and Statistics Directorate.

Mair, G. (2004) 'Diversionary and non-supervisory approaches to dealing with offenders', in Bottoms, A., Rex, S. and Robinson, G. (eds) *Alternatives to Prison: Options for an Insecure Society*, Cullompton: Willan.

Marshall, T. (1996) 'The evolution of restorative justice in Britain', *European Journal of Criminal Policy and Research*, 4 (4) pp.21–43.

Masters, G. (2002a) 'Family group conferencing: A victim perspective', in Williams, B. (ed.) *Reparation and Victim-Focused Social Work*, London: Jessica Kingsley Publishers.

Masters, G. (2002b) 'In or out? Some critical reflections upon the potential for involving victims of youth crime in restorative processes in England and Wales', *British Journal of Community Justice*, 1 (1) pp.99–110.

Mattinson, J. and Mirrlees-Black, C. (2000) *Attitudes to Crime and Criminal Justice: Findings from the 1998 British Crime Survey*, London: Home Office Research Development and Statistics Directorate.

Mawby, R. (2003) 'The provision of victim support and assistance programmes: A cross-national perspective', in Davies, P., Francis, P. and Jupp, V. (eds) *Victimisation: Theory, Research and Policy*, Basingstoke: Palgrave Macmillan.

Mawby, R. I. and Gill, M. L. (1987) *Crime Victims: Needs, Services, and the Voluntary Sector*, London: Tavistock.

Mawby, R. I. and Walklate, S. (1994) *Critical Victimology: International Perspectives*, London: Sage.

Maxwell, G. and Morris, A. (1993) *Family, Victims and Culture: Youth Justice in New Zealand*, Wellington, New Zealand: Social Policy Agency and Institute of Criminology, Victoria University.

Maxwell, G. and Morris, A. (2001) 'Family group conferences and reoffending', in Morris, A. and Maxwell, G. (eds) *Restorative Justice for Juveniles: Conferencing, Mediation and Circles*, Oxford: Hart.

Mayhew, P. and van Kesteren, J. (2002) 'Cross-national attitudes to punishment', in Roberts, J. V. and Hough, M. (eds) *Changing Attitudes to Punishment: Public Opinion, Crime and Justice*, Cullompton: Willan.

McCarthy, C. (2004) 'I no longer have to hide when I see him', *Observer*, Review Supplement, 21 November, p.4.

McCold, P. (2000) 'Towards a mid-range theory of restorative criminal justice: A reply to the maximalist model', *Contemporary Justice Review*, 3 (4) pp.357–414.

McCold, P. (2004) 'Paradigm muddle: The threat to restorative justice posed by its merger with community justice', *Contemporary Justice Review*, 7 (1) March, pp.13–35.

McConville, M. (2002) 'Plea bargaining', in McConville, M. and Wilson, G. (eds) *The Handbook of the Criminal Justice Process*, Oxford: Oxford University Press.

McEwan, J. (2002) 'Special measures for witnesses and victims', in McConville, M. and Wilson, G. (eds) *The Handbook of the Criminal Justice Process*, Oxford: Oxford University Press.

McIvor, G. (2004) 'Reparative and restorative approaches', in Bottoms, A., Rex, S. and Robinson, G. (eds) *Alternatives to Prison: Options for an Insecure Society*, Cullompton: Willan.

McLaughlin, E., Fergusson, R., Hughes, G. and Westmarland, L. (eds) (2003) *Restorative Justice: Critical Issues*, London: Sage.

McLaughlin, E. and Muncie, J. (2000) 'The criminal justice system: New Labour's new partnerships', in Clarke, J., Gewirtz, S. and McLaughlin, E. (eds) *New Managerialism, New Welfare?* London: Sage.

Meiners, R. E. (1978) *Victim Compensation*, Lexington, KY: D. C. Heath.

Miers, D. (2001) *An International Review of Restorative Justice*, Crime Reduction Research Series Paper 10, London: Home Office.

Miers, D., Maguire. M., Goldie, S., Sharpe, K., Hale, C., Netten, A., Uglow, S., Doolin, K., Hallam, A., Enterkin, J. and Newburn, T. (2001) *An Exploratory Evaluation of Restorative Justice Schemes*, Crime Reduction Research Series Paper 9, London: Home Office.

Ministry of Justice (1995) *Restorative Justice: A Discussion Paper*, Wellington, New Zealand: Ministry of Justice.

Moore, D. and Forsyth, L. (1995) *A New Approach to Juvenile Justice: An Evaluation of Family Conferencing in Wagga Wagga*, New South Wales: Charles Sturt University Centre for Rural Social Research.

Morgan, R. and Sanders, A. (1999) *The Uses of Victim Statements*, London: Home Office Research, Development and Statistics Directorate.

Morran, D., Andrew, M. and Macrae, R. (2002) 'Effective work with abusive men', in Williams, B. (ed.) *Reparation and Victim-Focused Social Work*, London: Jessica Kingsley Publishers.

Morris, A. (2002a) 'Critiquing the critics: A brief response to critics of restorative justice', *British Journal of Criminology*, 42 (3) pp.596–615.

Morris, A. (2002b) 'Shame, guilt and remorse: Experiences from family group conferences in New Zealand', in Weijers, I. and Duff, A. (eds) *Punishing Juveniles: Principle and Critique*, Oxford: Hart.

Morris, A. and Gelsthorpe, L. (2000) 'Something old, something borrowed, something blue, but something new? A comment on the prospects for restorative justice under the Crime and Disorder Act 1998', *Criminal Law Review*, January, pp.18–30.

Morris, A. and Maxwell, G. (2000) 'The practice of family group conferences in New Zealand: Assessing the place, potential and pitfalls of restorative justice', in Crawford, A. and Goodey, J. (eds) *Integrating a Victim Perspective in Criminal Justice*, Aldershot: Ashgate.

Morris, A.M., Maxwell, G. and Robertson, J. (1993) 'Giving victims a voice: A New Zealand experiment', *Howard Journal of Criminal Justice*, 32 (4) pp.304–21.

Muncie, J. (2003) 'Youth, risk and victimisation', in Davies, P., Francis, P. and Jupp, V. (eds) *Victimisation: Theory, Research and Policy*, Basingstoke: Palgrave Macmillan.

Munro, P. (2004) 'I mean business', *The Guardian*, G2 Supplement, 23 November, pp.16–17.

Murray, K. (1997) *Preparing Child Witnesses for Court: A Review of Literature and Research*, Edinburgh: Scottish Office Home Department Central Research Unit.

NAVSS (National Association of Victims Support Schemes) (1988) *The Victim in Court*, report of a working party convened by the National Association of Victims Support Schemes, chaired by Lady Ralphs, London: Victim Support.

Naylor, J. (2003) 'Circles of support', *Public Protection News* 5, pp.2–3.

Nellis, M. (2000) 'Creating community justice', in Pease, K., Ballintyne, S. and McLaren, V. (eds) *Key Issues in Crime Prevention, Crime Reduction and Community Safety*, London: IPPR.

Nelson, L. (2004) 'The development of a strategic approach to restorative justice – the issues for government', paper given at the European Forum for Victim–Offender Mediation and Restorative Justice conference, Budapest, October.

New Statesman (2004) *Community Justice: Concepts and Delivery, a Round-table Discussion*, special supplement, 8 December, http://www.newstatesman.co.uk/pdf/communityjustice 2003supp.pdf

Newburn, T. and Merry, S. (1990) *Keeping in Touch: Police–Victim Communication in Two Areas*, Research Study no.116, London: Home Office.

Newton, E. (2003) 'A study of the policies and procedures implemented by the probation service with respect to victims of serious crime', *British Journal of Community Justice*, 2 (1) 25–36.

Nugent, W. R., Williams, M. and Umbreit, M. S. (2003) 'Participation in victim–offender mediation and the prevalence and severity of subsequent delinquent behaviour: A meta-analysis', *Utah Law Review*, 1, pp.137–66.

Nuttall, M. and Morrison, S. (1997) *It Could Have Been You*, London: Virago.

O'Dea, P. (2000) 'Family conferences in the Children Bill, 1999', in the proceedings of a seminar, *The Children Bill, 1999*, Dublin: Children's Legal Centre.

O'Dwyer, K. (2001) *Restorative Justice Initiatives in the Garda Siochana: Evaluation of the Pilot Programme*, Templemore, Eire: Garda Research Unit.

O'Dwyer, K. (2004) Personal communication.

Osborne, D. and Plastrik, p.(2000) 'Repairing the social fabric', *The New Democrat*, 1 August, available at http://www.ppionline.org/ndol/print.cfm?contentid=1917

Pearce, F. and Tombs, S. (1997) 'Hazards, law and class: contextualizing the regulation of corporate crime', *Social and Legal Studies*, 6 (1) pp.79–107.

Pelikan, C. (1999) 'Mediation between the victim and the offender in Austria: Legal ramifications and practice', in Czarnecka-Dzialu, B. and Wojcik, D. (eds) *Juvenile Offender–Victim Mediation*, Warsaw: Institute of Justice/Oficyna Naukowa.

Pelikan, C. (2000) 'Victim–offender mediation in Austria', in European Forum for Victim–Offender Mediation and Restorative Justice (ed.) *Victim–Offender Mediation in Europe: Making Restorative Justice Work*, Leuven, Belgium: Leuven University Press.

Perry, J. (2004) 'Hate crime against people with learning difficulties: The role of the Crime and Disorder Act and *No Secrets* in identification and prevention', *Journal of Adult Protection*, 6 (1), pp.27–34.

Petrunik, M. G. (2002) 'Managing unacceptable risk: Sex offenders, community response, and social policy in the United States and Canada', *International Journal of Offender Therapy and Comparative Criminology*, 46 (4), pp.483–511.

Plotnikoff, J. and Woolfson, R. (1998) *Witness Care in Magistrates' Courts and the Youth Court*, Research Findings no. 68, London: Home Office Research and Statistics Directorate.

Pollard, C. (2000) 'Victims and the criminal justice system: A new vision', *Criminal Law Review*, pp.5–17.

Potter, K. (2004) 'We've come a long way...', *Victim and Witness View*, 1, November, pp.10–14.

Press Association (2004) 'Police arrest five over cockling deaths', *The Guardian*, 9 February, www.guardian.co.uk/uk_news/story/0,36014,1144094,00.html

Prinsloo, J., Naude, B., Ladikos, T., Snyman, R. and Ngwisha, J. K. (2001) 'The International Crime (Victim) Survey in Swaziland (1998)', *Acta Criminologica: South African Journal of Criminology*, 14 (1), pp.19–29.

Pritchard, J. (2001) (ed.) *Good Practice with Vulnerable Adults*, London: Jessica Kingsley Publishers.

Proeve, M. and Howells, K. (2002) 'Shame and guilt in child sexual offenders', *International Journal of Offender Therapy and Comparative Criminology*, 46 (6) pp.657–67.

Punch, M. (1996) *Dirty Business: Exploring Corporate Misconduct; Analysis and Cases*, London: Sage.

Pye, B. (2004) 'Cocklers' memorial speech', Gregson Centre, Lancaster, 2 April, http://virtual-lancaster.net/diversity/pye_speech.htm

QPSW (2003) *Circles of Support and Accountability in the Thames Valley, Interim Report November 2003*, London: Quaker Peace and Social Witness.

Raine, J. W. and Smith, R. E. (1991) *The Victim/Witness in Court Project: Report of the Research Programme*, London: Victim Support.

Rawlinson, P. (2002) 'Capitalists, criminals and oligarchs: Sutherland and the new "robber barons"', *Crime, Law and Social Change*, 37, pp.293–307.

Reeves, H. and Wright, M. (1995) 'Victims: Towards a reorientation of justice', in Ward, D. and Lacey, M. (eds) *Probation: Working for Justice*, London: Whiting and Birch.

Restorative Justice Consortium (2003) *Response to the Government's Strategy on Restorative Justice 2003*, London: RJC.

Retzinger, S. M. and Scheff, T. J. (1996) 'Strategy for community conferences: Emotions and social bonds', in Galaway, B. and Hudson, J. (eds) *Restorative Justice: International Perspectives*, Monsey, NY: Criminal Justice Press and Amsterdam: Kugler.

Roberts, J. V. and Edgar, A. (2003) 'Victim Impact Statements at sentencing: Perceptions of the judiciary in Canada', *The International Journal of Victimology*, 1 (4), http://www.jidv.com/ROBERTS,J-JIDV2003-1-(4).htm

Robinson, A. L. (2004) *Domestic Violence MARACs (Multi-Agency Risk Assessment Conferences) for Very High-Risk Victims in Cardiff, Wales: A Process and Outcome Evaluation*, Cardiff: School of Social Sciences, Cardiff University.

Roche, D. (2003) *Accountability in Restorative Justice*, Oxford: Oxford University Press.

Rock, P. (1990) *Helping Victims of Crime: The Home Office and the Rise of Victim Support in England and Wales*, Oxford: Clarendon.

Rock, P. (2004) *Constructing Victims' Rights: The Home Office, New Labour, and Victims*, Oxford: Oxford University Press.

Sampson, A. (2000) *Mandela: The Authorised Biography*, London: HarperCollins.

Sanders, A. (1999) *Taking Account of Victims in the Criminal Justice System: A Review of the Literature*, Edinburgh: Scottish Office Central Research Unit.

Sanders, A. (2002) 'Victim participation in an exclusionary criminal justice system', in Hoyle, C. and Young, R. (eds) *New Visions of Crime Victims*, Oxford: Hart.

Sanders, A. (2004) 'Involving victims in sentencing: A conflict with defendants' rights?' in Cape, E. (ed.) *Reconcilable Rights? Analysing the Tension between Victims and Defendants*, London: Legal Action Group.

Sanders, A., Hoyle, C., Morgan, R. and Cape, E. (2001) 'Victim Impact Statements: Don't work, can't work', *Criminal Law Review*, June, pp.447–58.

Sanderson, I. (2002) 'Evaluation, policy learning and evidence-based policy making', *Public Administration*, 80 (1) pp.1–22.

Shapland, J. and Bell, E. (1998) 'Victims in the Magistrates' Court and Crown Court', *Criminal Law Review*, 537–46.

Shapland, J., Willmore, J. and Duff, p.(1985) *Victims in the Criminal Justice System*, Aldershot: Gower.

Shearing, C. (2001) 'Transforming security: A South African experiment', in Strang, H. and Braithwaite, J. (eds) *Restorative Justice and Civil Society*, Cambridge: Cambridge University Press.

Sherman, L., Strang, H. and Woods, D. J. (2000) *Recidivism Patterns in the Canberra Reintegrative Shaming Experiments (RISE)*, Canberra: Centre for Restorative Justice, Australian National University, http://www.aic.gov.au/rjustice/rise/

Skelton, A. (2002) 'Restorative justice as a framework for juvenile justice reform: A South African perspective', *British Journal of Criminology*, 42 (3) pp.496–513.

Slapper, G. and Tombs, S. (1999) *Corporate Crime*, Harlow: Longman.

Smith, D. J. (2002) 'Crime and the life course', in Maguire, M., Morgan, R. and Reiner, R. (eds) *The Oxford Handbook of Criminology*, third edition, Oxford: Oxford University Press.

Spackman, P. (ed.) (2000) *Victim Support Handbook: Helping People Cope with Crime*, London: Hodder and Stoughton.

Sparks, R. (1994) 'Can prisons be legitimate?', *British Journal of Criminology*, 34 (1) pp.14–28.

Spencer, J. R. (2004) 'Criminal procedure: The rights of the victim, versus the rights of the defendant', in Cape, E. (ed.) *Reconcilable Rights? Analysing the Tension Between Victims and Defendants*, London: Legal Action Group.

Strang, H. (2002) *Repair or Revenge? Victims and Restorative Justice*, Oxford: Oxford University Press.

Strang, H. (2004) 'The threat to restorative justice posed by the merger with community justice: A paradigm muddle', *Contemporary Justice Review*, 7 (1) March, pp.75–9.

Tarrant, A. (2003) 'The sexual abuse of people with learning difficulties: The problem and possible solutions', *Journal of Adult Protection*, 5 (3) pp.6–13.

Tauri, J. and Morris, A. (1997) 'Re-forming justice: The potential of Maori processes', *Australian and New Zealand Journal of Criminology*, 30 (2) pp.149–67, and reproduced as

Chapter 4 of McLaughlin, E., Fergusson, R., Hughes, G. and Westmarland, L. (eds) (2003) *Restorative Justice: Critical Issues*, London: Sage.

Temkin, J. (1997) 'Plus ça change: Reporting rape in the 1990s', *British Journal of Criminology*, 37 (4) pp.507–28.

Temkin, J. (2002) *Rape and the Legal Process*, second edition, Oxford: Oxford University Press.

Tickell, S. and Akester, K. (2004) *Restorative Justice: The Way Ahead*, London: Justice.

Tombs, S. (forthcoming) 'Corporate crime', in Hale, C., Hayward, K., Wahidin, A. and Wincup, E. (eds.) *Criminology*, Oxford: Oxford University Press.

Tomlinson, H. (2004) 'Drugs giant moves trials abroad', *The Guardian*, 1 November, p.2.

Tudor, B. (2002) 'Probation work with victims of crime', in Williams, B. (ed.) *Reparation and Victim-Focused Social Work*, London: Jessica Kingsley Publishers.

Umbreit, M. (1999) 'Avoiding the marginalization and "McDonaldization" of victim–offender mediation: A case study in moving toward the mainstream', in Bazemore, G. and Walgrave, L. (eds) *Restoring Juvenile Justice: Repairing the Harm of Youth Crime*, Monsey, NY: Criminal Justice Press.

Umbreit, M. S. (2001) *The Handbook of Victim Offender Mediation: An Essential Guide to Practice and Research*, San Francisco, CA: Jossey-Bass.

Umbreit, M. S., Bradshaw, W. and Coates, R. B. (1999) 'Victims of severe violence meet the offender: Restorative justice through dialogue', *International Review of Victimology*, 6 (4) pp.321–43.

Umbreit, M. and Zehr, H. (2003) 'Restorative family group conferences: Differing models and guidelines for practice', in McLaughlin, E., Fergusson, R., Hughes, G. and Westmarland, L. (eds) *Restorative Justice: Critical Issues*, London: Sage. [First published in *Federal Probation*, 60 (3) pp.24–9, (1996)]

United Nations (1985) *Declaration of Basic Principles of Justice for Victims of Crime and Abuse of Power*, Geneva: UN (and at http://www.unhcr.ch/html/menu3/6/ h_comp49.htm).

United Nations (1999) *Handbook on Justice for Victims, On the Use and Application of the Declaration of Basic Principles of Justice for Victims of Crime and Abuse of Power*, New York, NY: United Nations Office for Drug Control and Crime Prevention.

United Nations (2000) *Basic Principles on the Use of Restorative Justice Programmes in Criminal Justice Matters*, http://pficjr.org/programs/un/canadaItaly

Ursel, J. (2002) '"His sentence is my freedom": The criminal justice processing of domestic violence cases in the Winnipeg family violence court', in Tutty, L. and Goard, C. (eds) *Reclaiming Self: Issues and Resources for Women Abused by Domestic Partners*, Black Point, Nova Scotia: Fernwood.

Van Ness, D. (2002) 'The shape of things to come: A framework for thinking about a restorative justice system', in E. G. M. Weitekamp and H.-J. Kerner (eds) *Restorative Justice: Theoretical Foundations*, Cullompton: Willan.

Van Stokkom, B. (2002) 'Moral emotions in restorative justice conferences: Managing shame, designing empathy', *Theoretical Criminology*, 6 (3) pp.339–60.

Victim Support (undated) *Magistrates' Court Witness Service Practice Manual*, London: Victim Support.

Victim Support (1995) *The Rights of Victims of Crime*, London: Victim Support.

Victim Support (2001) *Manifesto 2001*, London: Victim Support.

Victim Support (2002) *Criminal Neglect: No Justice Beyond Criminal Justice*, London: Victim Support.

Victim Support (2003) *Insult to Injury: How the Criminal Injuries Compensation System is Failing Victims of Crime*, London: Victim Support.

Victim Support (2004a) *30:30 Vision: Victim Support at 30 and the Challenges Ahead*, London: Victim Support.

Victim Support (2004b) *Victim Support Annual Report and Accounts 2003*, London: Victim Support.

Vulliamy, E. (2004) 'Majlinda was just 13 when she was snatched from her Albanian village and sold into the sex industry', *Observer*, Magazine, 3 October, pp.20–31.

Wainwright, M. (2004) 'Gangmasters may escape with light jail sentences', *The Guardian*, 9 February, www.guardian.co.uk/uk_news/story/o,3604,1143837,00.html

Walgrave, L. (2002) 'From community to dominion: In search of social values for restorative justice', in E. G. M. Weitekamp and H.-J. Kerner (eds) *Restorative Justice: Theoretical Foundations*, Cullompton: Willan.

Walklate, S. (1989) *Victimology: The Victim and the Criminal Justice Process*, London: Unwin Hyman.

Walklate, S. (2002) 'Victim Impact Statements', in Williams, B. (ed.) *Reparation and Victim-Focused Social Work*, London: Jessica Kingsley Publishers.

Walklate, S. (2003) *Understanding Criminology: Current Theoretical Debates*, second edition, Buckingham: Open University Press.

Walklate, S. (2004) 'Justice for all in the 21st century: The political context of the policy focus on victims', in Cape, E. (ed.) *Reconcilable Rights: Analysing the Tension between Victims and Defendants*, London: Legal Action Group.

Watt, N. (2004) 'Taking hard line against offenders still Howard's way', *The Guardian*, 11 August, p.4.

Wemmers, J.-A. (1996) *Victims in the Criminal Justice System*, Amsterdam: Kugler.

Wemmers, J.-A. (2002) 'Restorative justice for victims of crime: A victim-oriented approach to restorative justice', *International Review of Victimology*, 9 (1) pp.43–59.

Wilcox, A. (2003) 'Evidence-based youth justice? Some valuable lessons from an evaluation for the Youth Justice Board', *Youth Justice*, 3 (1) June, pp.19–33.

Wilcox, A. and Hoyle, C. (2002) *Final Report for the Youth Justice Board on the National Evaluation of Restorative Justice Projects*, Oxford: Centre for Criminological Research, University of Oxford.

Williams, B. (1999a) *Working with Victims of Crime: Policies, Politics and Practice*, London: Jessica Kingsley Publishers.

Williams, B. (1999b) 'The Victim's Charter: Citizens as consumers of criminal justice services', *Howard Journal of Criminal Justice*, 38 (4), pp.384–96.

Williams, B. (2000) 'Victims of crime and the new youth justice', in Goldson, B. (ed.) *The New Youth Justice*, Lyme Regis: Russell House.

Williams, B. (2001) 'Reparation orders for young offenders: Coerced apologies?', *Relational Justice Bulletin*, 9, January, p.8.

Williams, B. (2002) 'Counselling in legal settings: Provision for jury members, vulnerable witnesses and victims of crime', in Jenkins, P. (ed.) *Legal Issues in Counselling and Psychotherapy*, London: Sage.

Williams, B. (forthcoming) 'Victims', in Hale, C., Hayward, K., Wahidin, A. and Wincup, E. (eds) *Criminology*, Oxford: Oxford University Press.

Wilson, C. (2003) 'Circles of support and accountability: Thames Valley', in QPSW, *Circles of Support and Accountability in the Thames Valley, Interim Report November 2003*, London: Quaker Peace and Social Witness.

Wilson, M. (2003) *Perpetrator Programmes for Male Domestic Violence Offenders: What do we Know about Effectiveness?* Towards Effective Practice Papers 4, Edinburgh: Criminal Justice Social Work Development Centre for Scotland.

Wilson, R. J. and Picheca, J. E. (forthcoming) 'Circles of support and accountability: Engaging the community in sexual offender risk management', in Schwartz, B. (ed.) *The Sex Offender*, volume 5, Kingston, NJ: Civic Research Institute.

Women's Aid (2004) 'Women's Aid welcomes the Domestic Violence, Crime and Domestic Violence Act but will lobby for greater protection for women and children at risk', press release, London: Women's Aid, www.womensaid.org.uk/press_releases

Woolf, L. C. J. (2002) 'Achieving criminal justice', the 2002 Rose lecture given at Manchester Town Hall, 29 October, London: Lord Chancellor's Department Press Office, mimeo.

Woolf, Lord Justice and Tumim, Judge S. (1991) *Prison Disturbances, April 1990*, Cmd. 1456, London: HMSO.

Wright, M. (1991) *Justice for Victims and Offenders*, Milton Keynes: Open University Press.

Wright, M. (1996) *Justice for Victims and Offenders*, second edition, Winchester: Waterside Press.

Wright, M. (2000) 'Restorative justice: For whose benefit?', in European Forum for Victim–Offender Mediation and Restorative Justice (ed.) *Victim–Offender Mediation in Europe: Making Restorative Justice Work*, Leuven, Belgium: Leuven University Press.

Yantzi, M. (1998) *Sexual Offending and Restoration*, Waterloo, Ontario: Herald Press.

Yantzi, M. (2004) 'People, peace and possibilities', Community Justice Initiatives website, http://www.cjiwr.com/resources_article_1.html

Young, R. (2001) 'Just cops doing "shameful" business? Police-led initiatives in restorative justice and the lessons of research', in Morris, A. and Maxwell, G. (eds) *Restorative Justice for Juveniles*, Oxford: Hart.

Young, R. and Goold, B. (1999) 'Restorative police cautioning in Aylesbury – from degrading to reintegrative shaming ceremonies?', *Criminal Law Review*, February, 126–38, reprinted as Chapter 8 of McLaughlin, E., Fergusson, R., Hughes, G. and Westmarland, L. (eds) (2003) *Restorative Justice: Critical Issues*, London: Sage.

Youth Justice Board for England and Wales (2001) *Good Practice Guidelines for Restorative Justice Work with Victims and Young Offenders*, London: YJB.

Yun, G. (2004) *Chinese Migrants and Forced Labour in Europe*, Working Paper 32, Geneva: International Labour Office.

Zaubermann, R. (2000) 'Victims as consumers of the criminal justice system?', in Crawford, A. and Goodey, J. (eds) *Integrating a Victim Perspective within the Criminal Justice System*, Aldershot: Ashgate.

Zedner, L. (1995) 'Comparative research in criminal justice', in Noaks, L., Levi, M. and Maguire, M. (eds) *Contemporary Issues in Criminology*, Cardiff: University of Wales Press.

Zedner, L. (2002) 'Victims', in Maguire, M., Morgan, R. and Reiner, R. (eds) *The Oxford Handbook of Criminology*, third edition, Oxford: Oxford University Press.

Zehr, H. (1990) *Changing Lenses: A New Focus on Crime and Justice*, Scottdale, PA: Herald Press.

Zehr, H. and Mika, H. (2003) 'Fundamental concepts of restorative justice', in McLaughlin, E., Fergusson, R., Hughes, G. and Westmarland, L. (eds) *Restorative Justice: Critical Issues*, London: Sage. [First published in *Contemporary Justice Review, 1* (1) pp.47–56, (1997)]

Subject Index

Aboriginal cultures 60, 71–3, 93
apology 59, 62, 66, 76, 77, 79–80, 82, 130
Australia 34, 74, 147
    offenders' rights 66
    restorative justice and minorities 60, 71
    RISE project 70, 77–8
    victim statements 102–3
Austria 24, 60, 66, 78, 79

Belgium 65, 78, 111, 114–6, 133, 135, 152
Blair, Tony 91
British Journal of Community Justice 34

Canada 33, 60, 102
    circles of support and accountability 39–45
    family violence court 19
    victim–offender mediation 113–4, 133
    victim statements 100, 101, 102
child abuse 18, 20
child victims 109, 142, 143–4, 151
circle sentencing 59, 82
circles of support and accountability 39–45, 54–5, 59, 128
class 68, 96, 141
closure 76, 77, 96, 101, 104, 105, 113, 125, 130
commercial providers
    of social control services *see* private companies
    of training and consultancy 65
Commissioner for Victims and Witnesses 97
communitarianism 27–9, 63, 68
community justice 27–56, 128–9
    centres 33, 46–50, 128–9
    definition 32, 54
Community Reparative Boards (USA) 34–7, 55, 82, 129
community safety partnerships 53

compensation 24, 83, 90, 128, 139, 143, 148, 151–2
    enforcement 86, 146
    family group conferences and 76, 77
    history of 13–16, 128
    mediation and 78
    restorative justice and 130
    state criminal injuries compensation 93–101, 128, 131–2, 151
confidentiality 39, 43, 64, 118, 126
corporate crime, victims of 11, 94, 133, 138–43, 146
Council of Europe 94, 99, 107, 111, 135, 137
counselling 110, 113
courts 51, 67, 106, 121–2, 144, 145, 148
    specialist 19–20, 120
Crime and Disorder Act 1998 53, 67, 84
Crime Concern (UK NGO) 65
Criminal Justice Act
    1988 98
    2003 148
Crown Prosecution Service 11–12, 15, 22–3, 32, 48, 50–52, 103, 108
curfews 64
customary law 37, 93
Czech Republic 79

decarceration 34, 60, 76, 129
deferred sentences 49
Denmark 62, 79, 85
disabled people, as victims 143–4
domestic violence 51, 53, 117–9, 125, 133, 134
    and restorative justice 78
    see also courts, specialist; community justice centres
Domestic Violence, Crime and Victims Act 2004 17, 97, 142, 150
drug treatment and testing orders 48–9
Duluth model 117

empathy for victims 66–7, 80, 109, 114, 145–6
empowerment 112, 124–6
    community reparative boards and 36, 56
    domestic violence services and 118–9, 125

Author Index